THERE IS A TIME

There is a time in life, it seems,
for believing in dreams
THERE IS A TIME

Johnny Duhan

THERE IS A TIME

BRANDON

Published in 2001 by
Brandon
an imprint of
Mount Eagle Publications
Dingle, Co. Kerry, Ireland

ISBN 0 86322 283 8

10 9 8 7 6 5 4 3 2 1

Cover design: id communications, Tralee
Typesetting: Red Barn Publishing, Skeagh, Skibbereen
Printed by Omnia Books Ltd., Scotland

To my mother I owe the heart-
felt beat of my purest aim
that puts spirit in the word and soul
in the air; and, from my father,
the steady note that carries
the melodious theme of compassionate
love in my song.

A special thanks to Paddy Houlahan
for suggesting that I write this book
and for advice and encouragement along
the way. Thanks also to Peter Harkin,
John McKenna and Steve MacDonogh
for vital support.

Not forgetting Granny's Intentions.

Contents

"The Most Beautiful Girl in the World"   9

Daredevil   15

The Umbrella   21

The Pirates of Penzance   27

Eagle Tie   33

Ashes, Salt and Vinegar   41

Rolling Stones   49

The Intentions   55

The Foundry   61

The Go Go   67

"Band Lark"   73

Floored   79

The Sacrifice   85

Mary   91

Caged   97

The Revelles   105

Swinging London   113

Dave   121

Contents

The Launch   127

"I Just Want Us to Go On Having a Bit of Fun, That's All"   133

The Old House   139

Stray Dog   147

The Red Scarf   153

In Darkness   161

A Heavy Lunch in Frankfurt   167

Killala Bay   173

Alone   179

Back Home   185

Overlapping   193

The Knowledge   201

Ted's Vintage Rock'n'Roll Library   209

In Deep   215

The Brewery   221

The Room   229

Joyful Mystery   235

"The Most Beautiful Girl
in the World"

Sister, we're alone in the middle of the night
Counting car lights on the ceiling
Everything Will Be Alright

THE HARSH SOUND of my parents arguing downstairs woke me. I lay on my pillow looking up at the ceiling, trying to figure out what the row was about. The faint hum of an electric saw from Whelan's timber yard nearby made it hard to concentrate. I propped myself up in the bed and tried to listen more carefully. My sister Kay came into the bedroom, looking very worried. "Get up quick, Johnny. Something awful is going on downstairs. Mammy is acting very strange." She whispered this so as not to wake my three younger brothers sleeping in a set of two-tiered bunks opposite my single bed.

My parents went silent when Kay and I entered the kitchen. Though it was a bright summer morning, our small back window allowed only a little light into the room. I looked at my mother sitting in an armchair near the fireplace, then at my father standing with his back to the window. "What's going on? What's all the noise about?"

9

My father shoved his fingers through his hair. "It's nothing. Go back upstairs. We're just having a bit of an argument, that's all."

My mother raised her head and laughed. "Don't mind him. Stay where you are!"

I looked at her. Her eyes were blazing and her body movements were full of wild energy. Normally she was quiet and never made faces like this. I felt frightened and curious at the same time. "What's wrong with you, Mam?"

"There's nothing wrong with me, love. Your father's just been badgering me because I bought a copy of the Bible the other day. I wouldn't mind but I found him reading it last night himself, the hypocrite!"

My father rubbed his neck. "It wasn't just that. I'm worried about your health. You've been getting up at all hours of the morning again. You know what that led to in the past."

My mother jerked forward. "You're the one who put me away!"

My father took a deep breath. "I did it for your own good. I had to do it. You weren't well."

My mother glanced at Kay and me. "Don't worry, you two, I'm fine. I won't be leaving you again. I've never felt better in my life."

My father took a step towards my mother. "I know you're all right, love. You just need to rest, that's all."

"I don't need you telling me what to do!" My mother rose from her chair and started readjusting brass ornaments on the mantelpiece. While she was doing this, she gave me a peculiar smile. Then she turned and stared at my father with a twisted look on her face. "Do you know something? I love that boy over there far more than I ever loved you!"

I felt my heart catch in my chest and I found it hard to breath. My father tried to make light of the remark by laughing. This annoyed my mother. She started yelling at the top of her voice. My father tried to calm her down, but she became more and more hysterical. Kay started crying. My father asked us to go upstairs again, so we left the room.

In the hall Kay wiped her eyes with the bottom of her cardigan and said she was going to call on our sister Joan, who was staying at a friend's house in the neighbourhood. While she was heading for the front door I got my jacket from a hook in the hallway and left the house also.

Instinctively I started walking in the direction of the docks. Ten minutes later, I was sitting on a mooring bollard in the centre of the dockyard over-looking the Shannon river. I tried to put my confused thoughts in order but couldn't manage it. I kept thinking of what my mother had said and was unable to make sense of it.

The squeal of a low-flying gull made me shiver. I looked out over the wide river and began to cry. After a few moments, I pulled myself together and wiped my eyes with my fingers. I looked up river. My gaze came to rest on a line of sally trees on the left bank. This was a regular place where my friends and I went each year to chop down trees for the May bonfire. I remembered a fist fight I'd had there a few years before with Billy Moran after he said he'd heard that my mother had been in the "nuthouse". Though he was three years older than me, I gave him a black eye and a bloody nose.

A dredger started to leave the enclosed docks' area. I watched it make its way through the open sluice gates and chug a slow course out into the middle of the river, then my eyes drifted back to the docks. There was just one ship docked there, a black freighter. For a moment I forgot myself and thought of making my way down to where it was moored, to see where it was from and to check out what its cargo was. Checking out ships in the docks was a big hobby of mine, going back to when my father was a mer-chant seaman. Now, however, the new situation with my mother came back to me, so I put all thought of amusement out of my head.

My eyes drifted around the docks. I recalled the first time I had come here four or five years before. I was only six or seven years old at the time. My mother brought me down to see my father's ship coming in. It was a windy day. A black tam I was wearing blew off my head and ended up in the choppy water beside the ship as it was being moored. One of the offi-cers on board got a long pole with a hook at the end of it and fished the tam out of the water and held it out to my mother. Just as she was taking it from the hook, my father came on deck and waved to us. As soon as the gangplank was lowered, he came down on to the quay and kissed my mother. Then he brought me on board the ship and took me down to the engine room, where he worked as a maintenance engineer. When he returned me to my mother, he put his hands through her hair and told her that she was the most beautiful girl in Limerick. My mother laughed and pulled away from him. "Oh, so it's only Limerick now, is it? When we met first you told me I was the most beautiful girl in the world."

The dredger started hauling up its first load of mud in the centre of the river. The strain of the tightening pulleys and chains created a loud grating noise that echoed around the river area. Gulls and pigeons rose up from the water and hovered in the blue sky above the boat. I stood up and started making my way home.

Passing through Henry Street, I thought of going to the Redemptorist chapel to say a prayer for my mother. I went to a side shrine to the Sacred Heart and knelt down on the hard marble. My mother had great faith in the Sacred Heart. Some years before, she had developed a boil on the back of her neck that became so inflamed she had to take to her bed. The pain was so bad she asked me to go to the Sacred Heart shrine to say a prayer for her. I said the full five decades of the rosary. When I returned to the house, she was sitting up in bed with a smile on her face. The boil had burst, and she told me that her recovery was due to my prayers.

I looked up at the gold-framed picture of Jesus now and studied the exposed heart between the nail-pierced hands. The thorns around the heart and the tear-shaped blood-drops dripping from the deep gashes of the wounds made me shudder. I started praying, mechanically. I went through three Hail Marys, then stopped and couldn't go on. A lump came to my throat and tears ran down my nose. I looked around to see if anyone was looking at me. There wasn't. I tried to get back into the relief of crying but the tears wouldn't come. Again I thought of saying a few Hail Marys, but didn't have the heart for it. Instead I started talking to the picture below my breath. I poured out my heart to Jesus and begged Him to make my mother better. Then I got up from my knees and left the church.

When I arrived home, a friend of the family, Nancy O'Brian, broke the news to me that my mother had been taken to St Joseph's in an ambulance. She put her hand around my shoulder. "Don't fret, love, don't fret. Your father's with her. She'll be all right in a few days. Then we can go up and visit her."

A week went by before my mother was well enough to receive visitors. As the time approached for us to go and see her, I began to feel uneasy. It wasn't going to be like a normal visit to a hospital, as when my sister Pattie was in having her appendix out in Barrington's. St Joseph's I knew well. It was situated beside Limerick jail, just up the street from the Christian Brothers' school that my brothers and I attended. With a few classmates I had once climbed the back wall of the place to look inside. We spotted a few patients with crew-cuts and blank eyes. We laughed at them and called them "nutcases".

My father allowed only three of us accompany Nancy on the first visit; my sisters Joan and Kay, and myself. Once we entered the front gate and started making our way to the recuperating unit, my fear started to leave me. When my mother finally appeared before us, I was relieved to find that she didn't look like any of the patients I remembered from the past. She was tired looking and spoke with a slight slur, but otherwise she was her old self. She kissed and fondled our faces and told us that she'd be coming home soon. Nancy did most of the talking during the visit. But now that the ice was broken, I decided to return to the hospital by myself a few days later.

My second visit to St Joseph's was on a bright sunny day. My mother was delighted to see me. She took my hand and led me out into the sun. We walked around the grounds talking about home concerns. At one point, she asked me how my father was coping. "He's a good man, your father. Don't think he isn't. He's a very good man."

We came upon a small chapel. My mother suggested that we go in and say a prayer. As we were leaving the church, we were approached by a disturbed looking patient who put his hand out to my mother. He was drooling at the mouth and had a severe eye-twitch. My mother took a packet of Gold Flake cigarettes from her cardigan pocket and handed him two. "Make sure none of the others take the spare one from you, Tom."

On the way back to the ward, we came upon a grey building with barred windows, where some of the most disturbed patients in the hospital were kept. Because of the heat of the day, the windows were raised at the bottom. My mother went up to one of the dark openings and looked through the bars. A group of grey-haired women with bulging eyes clustered around the window, muttering and mumbling to themselves. My mother asked one of them to get Annie. A few moments later, a white-faced old lady with snow-white hair appeared at the bars, looking very agitated. When she spotted my mother, she smiled and grunted. My mother put her hand through the bars and touched her wrinkled hand. "I want you to meet my son, Annie. I told you about him before. He loves music, like yourself. Since he was a small boy he's never stopped singing."

The old woman glanced at me and grunted, then smiled at my mother. My mother turned to me. "Annie's a distant relation of yours on my side of the family. At one time she was considered one of the finest musicians in the city. She played the church organ. Shake her hand."

I reluctantly put my arm through the bars and took the old woman's hand. I could feel her bones through the wrinkled skin. She smiled at me and then turned to my mother and grunted. My mother touched her hand. "Look after yourself, Annie. I'll call and see you again tomorrow."

From the pebbled pathway, my mother glanced back at the barred window. "Annie's been here for years. None of her family visit her any more. You can't blame them, for she hardly recognises any of them. I don't think she realises I'm related to her, but I call to see her anyway. She's an angel. They're all God's angels up here."

DAREDEVIL

I'm up higher than the cross on the temple
DAREDEVIL

I T WAS GROWING dark, and there was still no sign of Uncle Jim. I went
upstairs for the third time and looked through our small back bedroom
window. Beyond the shadowy galvanised roof of Whelan's timber
yard, the top part of a lit-up Ferris wheel was revolving beneath the
first stars. To the left of the big wheel, a ladder outlined with coloured
lights was towering into the darkening sky, with the steeple of the
Redemptorist chapel behind it. A tremor of impatient excitement ran
through me. I cursed Uncle Jim for being late and went back downstairs.

In the kitchen my mother was changing the baby's nappy while at the
same time helping my brothers and sisters with their school homework. I
glanced at her and shook my head. "If he doesn't come soon, Dad'll be
home from work, and he won't let me go."

My mother took a safety pin from her mouth. "I told you not to get your
hopes up. You know how unreliable Jim is."

"But he promised he'd take me."

My brother Eric sniggered. "He's probably over in Reddan's getting
drunk."

My brother Michael looked up from his page. "Or over in Joe's with his sailor buddies."

My eldest sister Joan shook her head. "He's barred from Joe's after that time he took off his trousers there and walked up O'Connell Avenue in his underpants. I heard Daddy saying it."

Our nine-year-old sister Pattie broke into a fit of the giggles, and we all laughed along with her.

My mother shifted the baby on her lap. "Come on, get back to your homework. Your father will be home any minute, and I'll need the table for his supper."

Kay glanced in my direction. "What about Johnny? He hasn't opened a page all evening. He's been listening to the radio since he got in from school. He never does any homework, that fella."

My mother looked at me and shook her head. "It's true. I don't know what I'm going to do with you at all."

I glared at Kay. "Why don't you keep your trap shut, troublemaker!"

Kay was just about to snipe back at me but was interrupted by a knock at the front door. Joan and Michael rushed out to answer it. A few moments later, they returned to the kitchen hanging out of Uncle Jim's sleeve. Michael glanced at me, then looked up at Jim. "Please take me to the carnival, too, Uncle Jim. I'll be as good as gold, I swear."

Jim tapped Michael on the head. "I'd love to, Mikey, but you're too small. My own little fella's as old as you, and Mary wouldn't let me take him."

My mother looked at Jim and frowned. "I hope you haven't been drinking? I thought you said you'd be here at half seven?"

Jim wiped his mouth with the back of his hand. "I'm as sober as a judge. I got delayed downtown on a bit of business. But we're in lots of time. The daredevil's not due to dive till half nine."

My mother stood up with the baby in her arms. "Half *nine*? That's awful late. His father will have a fit."

Jim tightened the belt of his Macintosh and winked at me. "I'll have him back here before ten o'clock at the latest. I swear."

My mother handed the baby to Joan and started buttoning up my jacket. "Make sure you hold Jim's hand in the crowd. And if you get lost, go to the ticket office and tell someone."

Jim put his hand on my head. "Jesus Christ, he's eleven years of age!"

My mother took some silver coins from her purse and handed them to Jim. "Towards the rides. Don't be taking him into any bars. Go now before his father gets in."

Jim put his hand on my mother's arm. "It's great to see you making such steady progress, Chris. Don't be worrying your head. I'll look after him."

In the hall, my mother dipped her fingers in the holy water font on the wall and sprinkled my forehead. "Bless yourself, Johnny. And be a good boy, hear."

Walking down Wolfe Tone Street, Jim glanced in the direction of Reddan's Bar and rubbed his mouth. "How would you like a quick glass of lemonade? We still have lots of time."

I knew that if we went into Reddans' there would be no getting Jim out again. "Mrs Reddan might tell my mother that you brought me in."

Jim muttered under his breath and kept walking past the pub.

As we approached the carnival grounds on O'Connell Avenue, the crackling sound of Pat Boone singing 'Speedy Gonzales' could be heard playing at distortion level. I grabbed Jim's sleeve and tried to hurry him along. Jim held back, laughing. "Hold your horses, will you? It's not going to disappear."

Inside the brightly lit-up entrance gate, the carnival was buzzing with activity. Multi-coloured lights were swirling and swinging in so many different directions I didn't know where to look first. The high-pitched screams and loud laughter coming from the various amusements was thrillingly scary. I begged Jim to take me for a ride on the high-speed roundabouts, but he insisted that we inspect the large water tank that the daredevil was due to dive into first.

The tank turned out to be so high we couldn't see the water inside. Jim lifted me above his head, but the rim was still higher than my eye-level. I looked up at the narrow ladder rising up from the back of the tank and began to feel dizzy. "Is he really going to dive from way up there?"

Jim put me down. "Yeah, and he's going to be on fire when he does it. That's what the poster said."

"What if he misses the tank?"

Jim looked at the ground and laughed. "Splatter. Don't worry, I'll cover your eyes if that happens."

We took rides on the roundabouts, the dodgems and the chair-o-planes; then I coaxed Jim to take me on the Ferris wheel.

As the big wheel took us up in a quick backwards spin, butterflies rose up in my stomach and my body stiffened. Jim started rocking the seat backwards and forwards. I closed my eyes and begged him to stop. He put his arm around my shoulder and laughed. "I only want to heighten the thrill."

The wheel came to a sudden stop to allow people get off and others get on. I still had my eyes shut. Jim told me that we were right up on the top of the wheel. "Open your eyes and take a look. I've never seen the city looking so nice."

I eased my eyes open. The bright city below us was like a reflection of the starry sky above our heads. For a moment, I felt like we were suspended in outer space. I opened my eyes wider and gasped at the sparkling panorama. The wheel gave a sudden jerk and started turning again.

After we got off the Ferris wheel, Jim looked at his watch and said that it was time to take up our position for watching the daredevil.

At the front of the water tank, a large group of people were gathered. We stood back from edge of the crowd, where Jim said we'd have a better view of the dive. Jim lit a cigarette and looked at his watch again. "It won't be long now. It's just gone half nine."

Ten minutes went by and there was still no sign of the daredevil. People in the crowd began to grow restless. A bald-headed man in front of us with two young girls by his side glanced back at Jim and shook his head. "It's not fair on the young ones. They need to get home to their beds."

Jim rubbed his mouth. "I have an appointment myself at ten o'clock. At this rate, I won't get there before closing time."

A spotlight flashed over our heads and picked out the daredevil emerging from a caravan twenty or thirty feet away from the left hand side of the tank. He was dressed in purple leotards with a black cape. As he made his way towards the tank, brass-band music burst over the speakers. A wave of excitement ran through the crowd. I stood on the tips of my toes to get a better view.

At the front of the tank, the daredevil took off his cape and handed it to an assistant; then he stepped back to the ladder and took a bow. The crowd broke into a round of applause. The music stopped, and a crackling voice came over the speakers asking us to remain as quiet as possible while the daredevil was climbing the ladder. "This is a highly dangerous exercise, ladies and gentlemen. We would appreciate your full cooperation."

A slow tom-tom beat came over the speakers. The daredevil started climbing the narrow steps slowly, kicking his feet out like a ballet dancer before mounting each rung. When he reached the top of the ladder, he raised his hand and waved down at the crowd. Behind his head, an almost full moon was glowing like a bright halo. At the side of the moon, the dark cross of the Redemtorist' steeple was just about visible below a cluster of yellow stars. I began to grow dizzy looking up, so I lowered my eyes. Jim patted me on the head. "Look! They're going to set the pool on fire now. See the man with the torch."

At the front of the tank, an assistant climbed a few steps with a lighted torch and held it suspended above the rim of the water. The tom-tom music stopped and the PA system started crackling. "Would the people at the front of the crowd stand back as far as possible as we are about set the pool on fire."

The crowd shuffled back, and the assistant lowered the torch into the pool. An immediate blaze rose up and spread across the top of the tank. A loud gasp went up from the crowd. I stood up on my toes again. Faces at the front of the tank were lit up in a golden glow. Murmurs of excitement went up all around us. The speakers crackled again. "Ladies and gentlemen, can I have your undivided attention please! You are about to witness a unique experience: a death-defying dive by one of the world's leading highdive artists from a towering height never attempted before in this country. Will you put your hands together please for South America's daredevil supreme, Jose Crespi."

A loud round of applause rose and faded in the night breeze; then a drum roll came over the speakers and filled the air with tension. All eyes were on the dark figure swaying at the top of the ladder. The drum roll stopped and there was complete silence. Then the daredevil suddenly became a living flame. In an instant he leaned forward and dived head first. As the streak of fire plunged downwards, a loud gasp went up from the crowd. For a moment time seemed to stand still. My heart was in my mouth, and my hands were clasped together in a tight grip. A loud splash broke the silence. Jets of water flew up in the air, and the fire in the tank was extinguished. For a few moments, there was dead silence again, as the crowd waited to see if the daredevil had survived the dive. Suddenly his face appeared above the rim of the pool. Then he raised his arm and a huge round of applause went up in the crowd. I looked up at Jim and laughed. "My God! That was brilliant, absolutely brilliant!"

Jim smiled. "I told you it was going to be good. Jesus, to have a nerve like that! That's what life is all about, taking risks just for the thrill of it. Most of us are too frightened. Including myself."

The daredevil put on his cloak and started heading back to his caravan. Jim looked at his watch and rubbed his mouth. "Christ, look at the time. I'd better get you home fast or my brother'll have my life."

When we arrived at the house, Jim left me at the front door. "I won't go in. I'm late for my appointment as it is. I hope you had a good time?

I looked up at Jim and widened my eyes. "Tonight was the best night of my life!"

THE UMBRELLA

I sing for the lovers, the drunks, whose high aim like that of monks
Is to rise above the weight of man's heavy earthly state
MY GRAVITY

WHEN I ANSWERED the knock at the front door, there was a policeman standing outside.

"Is this Duhans'?"

"Yes, Guard."

"Is your father or mother home?"

"My father's at work and my mother's downtown shopping. Will I get one of my sisters?"

The guard smiled. "That won't be necessary. Just tell your father when he comes home that his brother James is up in Edward Street Garda barracks, charged with an offence. Your father will know what to do. Will you remember that?"

"I will, Guard. Is he locked up?"

The guard hesitated. "He is, son, and he might be kept in overnight. Don't forget to tell your father now."

I told my sisters what had happened; then I left the house and made my way to the clothing factory where my father worked. I entered the building by the back gate and found my father in the boilerhouse, sitting reading the racing page of a daily newspaper with his back to the main boiler. He seemed embarrassed to be caught resting on the job.

"Hey, matey, I'm on my tea break. I thought I told you before not to be calling here. The boss doesn't like me having social visits."

"I had to come, Dad. A guard was at the house about Uncle Jim."

My father threw his newspaper on a wooden box and walked over to the main boiler. "What's he done this time?"

"I don't know, but the guard said they might keep him locked up for the night."

My father cursed, something he rarely did. "I told him the last time he got into trouble that I wasn't going to bail him out any more, and I'm sticking to my guns!"

"But you can't just leave him up there, Dad! It wouldn't be right."

My father started reading one of the pressure clocks. "Yes, I can, and I'm going to. Now go on home, son. I'll see you later."

"But, Dad. . ."

"But nothing! Do as you're told! I'm not going up for him, and that's that!"

I stood for a moment staring at my father, then I shook my head and left the building.

I took a different route back to our street, cutting through People's Park. While I was walking along one of the narrow flower-bordered paths, one of my oldest memories of Jim came back to me. Out of the blue one day, he came swaying into our house with a knapsack on his back, just home from sea. My father was away at the time, but my mother made Jim feel at home. She cooked him a fry and told him all the local gossip. After the meal, Jim put me sitting on his knee and started singing. *We're on the one road sharing the same load. We're on the road to God knows where. . .* When the song ended, he dipped his hand into his knapsack and pulled out a bunch of green bananas, telling me that they had come all the way from a jungle in Ghana. My mother laughed and asked him if he was sure he hadn't stopped off at Mulrooney's fruit warehouse near the Harbour Bar on his way up from the docks, but Jim swore that he had picked the bananas with his own hands in the wilds of Africa.

Halfway through the park, I decided to go to the Garda barracks myself to let Jim know that my father wouldn't be coming to see him.

Before entering the police station on Edward Street, I took a deep breath. I had been inside the barracks once before a few years earlier after a friend and I were caught exploring an old abandoned school building in Perry Square, where a large quantity of lead went missing. My father believed me when I told him that I had nothing to do with the robbery, but he still marched me up to the Garda barracks and made me explain what I was doing in the building to one of the guards on duty. The guard filled a foolscap page with my story; then he took me on a tour of the cells at the back of the barracks. I took the whole thing very seriously until I spotted my father winking at the guard just before we left the station.

There were two policemen in the office now, one standing by a window drinking a mug of tea, the other sitting behind a desk reading a document. I walked up to the desk and cleared my throat. "Excuse me, Guard, I've come about Jim Duhan."

The guard lowered the page he was reading and looked at me. "And who might you be?"

"Jim Duhan's my uncle. A guard came to our house asking that my father come up here, but he can't get off work. I just want to get my uncle that message."

The guard looked across the room. "Is that the man Sheehan brought in this morning before I came on duty, Toomey?"

"It is, Sergeant. James Duhan. Apprehended for shoplifting in Todd's. He was intoxicated at the time. He put up some resistance when the security man tried to stop him from walking out the door with an expensive umbrella. Sheehan went down to bring him in, and he also called to his brother's house to let him know of the arrest when he was going off duty."

The sergeant looked at me sympathetically. "Would you like to talk to your uncle?"

"I would, Guard."

"Toomey, take this boy down to see his uncle. Give him five minutes in the cell with him. And you needn't wait with them."

I followed the guard down a dark hallway. We came to the familiar cells. I drew a deep breath while the guard was opening one of the heavy doors with a large key. Inside, my uncle was standing by a barred, frosted window with a troubled look on his face. Without locking the door, the guard left us and went back to the office.

Jim limped towards me. "Where's your father? Did he not get my message?"

"He can't get off work. The main boiler is broken down or something, and he's needed at the factory."

"Does he not know the trouble I'm in? There's been a terrible mistake. They think I tried to steal a brolly downtown, but I just walked out of the shop with it by mistake. I thought it was one of my own."

I looked at Jim's thin face. His lips were cracked and dry, and his left eye had a small cut over the eyebrow. His clothes were clean but crumpled and creased. "What happened to your leg?"

Jim looked down at his foot. "The man who stopped me in the shop kicked my legs from under me. I got a right knock."

"How long have you been here?"

Jim looked around the bare cell, and his eyes began to water. "Hours! And they say they're going to hold me overnight if someone doesn't bail me out. I can't stand confined spaces. I tried to tell the guard, but he wouldn't listen to me."

I looked at the single iron bed in a corner of the cell. It took up almost a third of the room. There was a fly walking on the grey pillow. I watched it for a moment, then turned back to Jim. His mouth was crooked and he was squeezing his hands.

"Would you like me to call to your house on my way home to let Aunt Mary know where you are?"

Jim panicked. "No, no, don't do that! I don't want her worrying about me. I've worried her enough as it is."

"But won't she be more worried if you don't go home tonight?"

Jim shook his head. "Your father will come and get me out, I know he will. Tell him I'm in a bad way when he gets in from work. Then he'll come up."

"But it might be very late before he gets in. Maybe he won't be able to come tonight."

Jim looked at me suspiciously. "He'll come all right. I know he will. He has a good heart, your father. He always looked after our mother when he was at sea. He sent money home regularly before he got married. And he stuck by your own mother, too, when the going got tough."

"What do you mean?"

Jim hesitated. "Nothing. I just meant that he has a good heart, that's all. He's helped me out more times than I care to remember. He'll bail me out this time, too. I know he will."

The guard came back to the cell. I felt relieved that I wasn't going to have to lie any more.

On my way home, I passed Jim's terraced house at the top of Caloney Street. I had been in there once with my father while Jim was on one of his binges. My father handed Aunt Mary an envelope. She was embarrassed accepting it. She thanked my father and put it in the pocket of her apron. Then she invited us into the back garden, where she picked a bunch of lilac and some other flowers for my mother. Holding the flowers awkwardly in his hand, my father looked around the neat garden and laughed. "Jim was never great for keeping a job, but he always had green fingers. He should have been a gardener, not a sailor."

When I arrived home, I found my mother washing clothes at the kitchen sink. Behind her, my sisters and brothers were reading books and comics at the table. Joan and Kay had told her about the guard calling to the house about Jim. I filled her in on my father's reaction to the news and started telling her of my visit to the Garda barracks. "The sergeant was nice. He let me visit Jim in his cell."

My mother stopped scrubbing the clothes and stared at me. "You mean you went up to the station all by yourself?"

"I had to; Dad wouldn't go. He just went on working as though nothing had happened."

My mother rubbed her forehead with the back of her wet hand. "Don't criticise your father! He has done more for that man than anyone I know. It's his own fault he's up there. It's poor Mary and the children I feel sorry for."

I sat beside Kay at the table, pushing her library book out of my way. "I still think it's wrong to leave him up there!"

Kay gave me a hard look. "Don't push my book around, you! Daddy is perfectly right not to go up for him. He's disgraced our family name all over town."

I glared at Kay. "You have no heart, do you know that?"

Joan looked at me. "Don't say that; it's not true. You weren't with us when he came up to us on the street blind drunk and made a show of us in front of all our friends."

25

Kay started to cry and upset our brother Barry, who began to bawl his head off. In the middle of this confusion, my father arrived home from work earlier than usual. The crying stopped. My mother finished her work at the sink and started setting the table for tea. My father washed his hands in grim silence, then took his place at the head of the table.

While he was putting mustard on a beef sandwich, he looked across the room at my mother. "I suppose you've heard the news?"

My mother nodded. "It's terrible."

"There's no way I'm going up for him this time!"

My mother poured tea into my father's cup. "You've done all you can for him. Maybe you could call on Mary. She'll be eaten up with worry if he doesn't go home tonight."

"I'll go up after I finish this."

Joan turned to my father. "Johnny was up at the Garda barracks."

My father stopped eating and glared at me. "Were you?"

I drew a breath. "I just wanted to let Jim know you wouldn't be going up, that's all."

My father shook his head. "You shouldn't have done that without asking my permission."

"I'm sorry, Dad."

My father ran his fingers through his hair. "How was he?"

"Worried looking."

"What's he up there for?"

I cleared my throat. "They say he tried to steal an umbrella, but he says it's all just a mistake."

My father gave a false laugh. "That's the story of his life."

I sat forward. "He still thinks you're going to go up for him, Dad."

My father's face grew as stiff as iron. "Well, he'll be a long time waiting. Now hurry up, you, and have your tea, and then get out your books and start doing your homework. You have important exams coming up soon."

THE PIRATES OF PENZANCE

I remember the nettled brain of my youth
Struggling with the roots of grammar
And the tough planters
CULTIVATION

W HEN THE BELL started ringing, I immediately hopped down from the wall dividing our school from the Presentation girls' convent school and raced up the yard as fast as I could. I took my place at the back of the long line of boys filing into the main building and made sure not to look in the direction of the principal, Brother Brick.

As usual, I felt a sinking of the heart as I climbed the three flights of stairs to the sixth grade classrooms. On the second floor, I looked through one of the stairway windows out into the rectangular yard we'd just come from and noticed a small boy, a latecomer, running towards the second grade classrooms at the bottom of the play area. My heart went out to him, thinking of the punishment he was likely to get for being late.

When we reached the top of the building, I followed Joe Hanrahan into classroom D, keeping my head down and my gaze away from the dark figure of Brother Dom, hovering in front of the blackboard. I took my place

27

as quietly as I could beside Paul Meehan and stuffed my brown canvass bag into the narrow compartment below my desk. Then I sat back and rummaged in my jacket pockets for a quencher sweet to suck on. When the shuffling noise of the other boys getting into their desks died down, Dom stepped forward and started blessing himself. *"In ainm an Athar agus an Mhic agus an Spioraid Naoimh, amen."*

After the morning prayers, Dom put his hands behind his back and started walking the aisles between the desks with a sour look on his face. "Right! Get out your English copies quickly and quietly. And God help anyone who hasn't got his composition done. Duhan! Take that sweet out of your mouth and stop fixing your hair, you nancy boy."

The class broke into a loud laugh, and a number of boys glanced in my direction with wide grins on their faces. As I had only been scratching my head, a wave of resentment rose up inside me. I stared at Dom defiantly but kept my mouth shut, knowing only too well that defending myself might mean four or five sharp swipes of the leather strap that he kept in the deep pocket of his black soutane. Dom stared back at me until I took the sweet from my mouth; then he turned his attention to Jimmy Moran.

"OK, Moran, we'll begin with you today. Start reading. And for God sake, take your time and don't swallow you tongue."

Moran stood up nervously and took a deep breath. "It wa-wa-wa-was a fi-fi-fi-fi-fine suh-suh-sunny day. We seh-seh-seh-set out foh-foh-for the rih-rih-rih-rih-river. . ."

While Willie was painfully stammering out the first few sentences of his composition on "A Day's Fishing on the Shannon", a timid knock came to the door. Dom told Willie to keep reading and went to answer it. All eyes in the room shifted to the door. A small, fair-haired boy swaying on his feet looked up nervously at Dom and whispered something in a voice too low for us to hear; then he turned on his heels and walked away. All eyes in the room turned back to Willie.

"I goh-got a woh-woh-worm from moh-moh-my cah-can and puh-put it oh-oh-on my huh-hook ah-and. . ."

Dom stepped back to the front of the classroom and glanced in my direction. "That's enough, Moran. Duhan! Brother Brick wants to see you in his office straight away. I wonder what kind of trouble you're in this time. Come on, come on, get a move on and don't keep *an príomhoide* waiting. He's a busy man, you know."

Going out the door, I glanced over my shoulder at Dom's back and pulled a long face. A few of the boys covered their mouths to stop themselves from laughing. Dom's head shot round, but I managed to close the door before he had time to say anything.

As I made my way down the narrow corridor to the principal's office, I racked my brain trying to think of what I might have done wrong. I had been sent to Brick's office on many occasions down the years, so I knew firsthand of his famous set of leather straps, graded in size to match a wide range of offences. When I reached his door, I took a deep breath and gave two gentle knocks. Instead of roaring his usual *"Tar isteach"*, Brick surprisingly came and opened the door himself. "Come in, John, come in." The smile on his face put me somewhat at ease, but I was suspicious at the same time. I took a couple of hesitant steps into the room and stood my ground. Brick went and sat behind his desk and looked at me over the wide rims of his glasses. "Take a seat, take a seat." He indicated a chair right in front of his desk and then sat back and put his hands behind his head.

As I sat down, I glanced at some of the things on his desktop – a bundle of *Our Boys* magazines, a number of opened and unopened letters, a box of chalk, a few biros and pencils. On the wall behind his head, an iron crucifix was set between a road safety poster (similar to one hanging in all the classrooms in the school) and a large map of Ireland divided into different coloured counties.

Brick took his hands from the back of his head and leaned forward. "How is Brother Dominic treating you these times – good, I hope? You won't feel it now till the exams; then you'll be deserting us for the secondary. You do intend going on to complete your education at secondary level, don't you?"

"Yes, sir, if I pass the entrance exam."

"You should have no bother there, if you apply yourself. I was looking up your past record. You started out in this school in class B. I don't know how you dropped to D, but many of our pupils from that grade have gone on to secondary level in the past. I hope you will as well. A good education is the foundation to a successful life. You'll understand that better when you go out into the world to make your own way."

I looked at some grease stains and ingrained chalk marks around the silver *fáinne* on the lapel of Brick's black jacket and shifted uneasily in my chair.

Brick readjusted his glasses and smiled. "There's no need to be afraid. I didn't call you here for anything you've done wrong. I know we've had our differences in the past, but that's water under the bridge now as far as I'm concerned. Let bygones be bygones is my motto. By the way, how is your father keeping these times?"

"Fine, sir."

Six months earlier, my father had come to the school to complain to Brick because of a severe beating I had received from Dom. Brick defended Dom and sneered at my father's demand for an apology. A heated row developed, and my father ended up calling Brick a tyrant. "If you weren't wearing that collar, I'd take you outside and teach you a lesson in manners!"

I looked at Brick now, wondering if he had forgotten my father's parting words to him. Brick picked up a biro from his desk and started twirling it between his fingers. "They tell me you have a mighty singing voice, John. Brother Joe never stops singing your praises. You've performed before his class a few times, I believe?"

"Yes, sir, last year."

Brick tapped the biro on his desk. "There's nothing like a good singer and a good song. If music be the food of love, play on, as Shakespeare so marvellously put it. I love music myself, always have done ever since I was a boy. My father was an accomplished musician. He played the fiddle, traditional music mainly. And my mother – God rest her – had a beautiful soprano voice. She sang for the local choir, but she was for ever singing popular music around the house, too. Jeanette McDonald, that kind of thing. But I won't keep you in suspense about why I called you here." He laid the biro beside the box of chalk. "To raise funds for some school equipment that's badly needed, we're putting on a bit of a show in the school hall after Easter – that wonderful production by Gilbert and Sullivan, *The Pirates of Penzance*. It's a marvellous show with some lovely melodic songs; one of the finest of their operettas, in my opinion. Very high-spirited stuff. Full of gaiety and laughter. It's mainly the secondary boys from first and second year that are involved in the cast, but they're a little lame in the singing department. And that's where you come in. You're tall enough and you're a good-looking boy. You'll do famously as one of the leads. Who knows, you might even end up being the star of the show. Rehearsals are already under way, but that's no problem. Brother Michael – the production manager – will be able to slot you in easily enough. It'll mean a lot of free classes, but don't worry about that. I'll talk to Brother Dominic about it. He might be able to fit you in with some individual tuition in his spare time to make up for the classes you'll miss. We mustn't lose sight of your exams, after all. Well, what do you say?"

Brick sat back in his chair and folded his arms.

I thought about the benefit of the free class time and was tempted, but then I pictured Dom giving me private tuition and stiffened in the chair.

"I'm sorry, sir, but I don't think I'd be much use to you. I'm only good at singing rock'n'roll music. I know nothing about Gilbert and Sullivan."

Brick's expression hardened. "That doesn't matter. A good singer should be able to sing any type of music, no matter what the style."

I looked down at my hands, remembering how Dom had flogged me till I'd cried in front of the whole class; then I glanced at Brick and recalled the humiliating way he had sneered at my father in front of me. I drew a deep breath and sat up in the chair. "It's not a question of not being able to sing it, sir. It's just that that type of music doesn't interest me. And I'd really prefer not to sing it."

Brick's right eye began to twitch and he gritted his teeth. "Something very sinister is going on in society when little pups like you can brazenly get away with insolence like this. But it's your mothers and fathers I blame. In these so-called prosperous times we live in, parents seem to have abrogated all responsibility to bringing up their children with even a modicum of common decency." He paused and took a loud breath, then glared at me. "Get up out of that chair and get back to your classroom, you little upstart!"

As I was leaving the office, he called me back. "One last thing. If you do happen to fail the forthcoming exams, have you any idea what you're going to do then?"

I hesitated. "No, sir, I haven't thought about it."

Brick scratched his ear. "Maybe it wouldn't be a bad idea to start thinking about it. It's always good to be prepared. Go on now, get back to your class."

I stood for a moment, then reached for the door handle and turned it the wrong way.

EAGLE TIE

Love is a delicate thing when it first comes round
Think of gentle wings above hard ground
When I met Margaret time started to fly
In the sky-blue of her eye
MARGARET

I T WAS FRIDAY night. The kitchen was full of steam. A large pot of water on the gas cooker was beginning to boil. My mother took it from the ring and carefully poured it into the steel tub in the centre of the floor. Gauging the temperature with her elbow, she told my sister Pattie to get into the bath, warning her not to splash the water. Beside the tub, my sister Joan was drying our three-year-old brother Barry, who had already had his bath; while over at the sink my father, just in from work, was shaving and singing 'Ramona'.

Having washed and changed my clothes earlier, I was waiting for my father to finish up at the sink so that I could use the mirror above the basin to straighten my necktie, which had an eagle on the front that was hard to position properly.

"Are you going to be there all night, Dad?"

"What's your rush, matey?"

My mother looked up at my father from the steaming tub. "He's going to a *céilí* in the Crescent tonight. I thought I told you about it the other day?"

My father glanced over his shoulder at me. "Is that tonight? Well, you'd better be on your best behaviour. No blackguarding, hear! By the way, is that one of my ties you're wearing? Who gave you permission to take that?"

My mother wiped her forehead with the back of her hand. "I told him he could borrow it, if he's real careful with it. But I think he needs a hand with the knot."

When my father finished shaving, he came over and readjusted the knot so that the eagle was evenly positioned halfway down my shirt-front. Then he stood back and looked me up and down. "You're a real swank now, matey. But take good care of that tie. That's one of my best. I got that in New Orleans when I was docked there one time. I could tell you stories about that tie."

My father had in fact already told me a story about how he had come by the tie a few years before. It involved a one-eyed black man who, having lost all his money to my father in a poker game in a bar in New Orleans, took off the fancy tie he was wearing and placed it in the kitty instead of a dollar wager. My father reluctantly accepted the tie as part of the bet and went on to win the hand outright. On scooping in the pool of his winnings, he offered to return the tie to the black man, but he refused to take it.

I got out the shoe polish and started polishing my winkle-pickers. When my sister Kay saw me with the brush in my hand, she came over and took it from me. "Give me that, clumsy, or you'll get polish all over Dad's good tie."

While I was combing my hair, there was a loud knock at the front door. I could tell by the force of the rap that it was Hearn. While Joan went to answer it, I slipped into my pointed shoes and grabbed my jacket from the back of a chair. As I was leaving the kitchen, my mother called after me: "Don't forget to bless yourself with holy water. And make sure to be in before eleven, hear!"

I bumped into my brothers, Eric and Michael, in the hall outside the sitting room. Eric looked down at my pointed shoes and sneered. "It's a *céilí* you're going to, not a hop!"

Michael stared at my tight pants and laughed. "Your balls must be squashed to death in them things, but they look deadly. How did you get into them?"

I tapped Michael on the head. "That's a secret. I'll tell you when you're bigger."

At the front door, Joan was talking to Hearn in a low voice. When she spotted me, she went silent and moved aside to let me pass. As I stepped out the door, I glanced back at her, then turned to Hearn. "What's she been saying to you?"

Hearn grinned. "She was just asking me to make sure you don't get off with some tart tonight. As if you'd get tarts in the Jezz."

Joan gave me an embarrassed look. "Don't mind him."

I laughed. "He's the one who goes for the tarts, not me."

Walking down Wolfe Tone Street, Hearn took a cigarette butt from the top pocket of his jacket and lit it. "I wish it was a real dance we were going to. I can't stand those diddle-e-di-di *céilí* bands. You can't jive to them. I'm only going here for your sake, I hope you know that."

Though Hearn was five or six inches smaller than me, he was three years older than I was. He was already attending the three big dance halls in town – the Stella, Cruise's and the Jetland – and he was for ever boasting to me about it.

When we arrived at the Jesuit hall on the Crescent, the *céilí* was in full swing. The doorman gave our drainpipes and winklepickers a crooked look when we handed him our tickets but he didn't stop us from entering the place. Inside, the dancefloor was teeming with lively dancers, hopping and jigging to the swift fiddles, accordions and drums of the céilí band on stage. Down one side of the hall, groups of fellas were gaping across at groups of girls standing and sitting by the opposite wall.

I followed Hearn to the front of the stage and looked up at the band. A bald-headed accordion player with a beetroot-coloured face was swaying backwards and forwards in front of a silver microphone, his fingers flying up and down the keys and buttons of his gold-spangled instrument at terrific speed. Beside him, a pot-bellied drummer with a toothy grin was rolling a steady rhythm on a snare drum, transferring his rattling sticks to a cow bell and high-hat when the two fiddlers at the front of the stage changed tempo.

Hearn glanced up at the drummer and sniggered, then turned away from the stage and looked up towards the girls' side of the hall.

"Do you see that bit of stuff up there by the radiator? The one in the pink dress with the big knockers? I'm gettin' up with her. You'll be all right on your own, won't you?"

"Sure."

Hearn swaggered across the floor and started jiving with a girl a little smaller than himself. Their dance movements were completely out of step with the rhythm of the Irish music. I began to feel embarrassed watching them, so I moved back up the hall and stood near the mineral bar.

One dance set came to an end and another started.

Among the first couples on to the floor, I noticed a small blonde-haired girl dancing with a fella who looked like he was going to trip over himself. The girl was dancing in perfect time to the music, but she kept putting her hand up to her mouth to stop herself from laughing at her awkward partner. Every now and then she flicked her hair back over her shoulder and raised her chin. I couldn't take my eyes off her. At the end of the set, she went and sat with a group of girls directly opposite where I was standing. The moment the band struck up another tune, I rushed over and asked her to dance.

Out on the floor I felt self-conscious taking my first few dance steps. "I haven't had much experience of this kind of dancing, I'm afraid."

The girl smiled. "I'm pretty basic myself when it comes to jigs and reels. But look around you; so's everyone else. Just bob and bounce like I'm doing and you'll be fine. You have good rhythm, anyway. I can see that."

"You're a very good dancer yourself. I've been watching you."

The girl lowered her eyes. "Thanks. My name's Margaret, by the way."

"Mine's John, but my friends call me Johnny."

While we were dancing Margaret noticed my tie. "I like the bird. Very fancy. Is it a hawk?"

"An eagle."

Margaret took the tie in her hand and started studying the bird. "It looks like it was hand-embroidered. Look at the red rhinestone for the eye. It's like a ruby. It's lovely. But it's a fierce looking creature, isn't it? The way the beak curves and the piercing way the red eye looks at you."

I looked into Margaret's eyes. They were bright blue, the colour of the sky on a sunny day. "Eagles are predators. They fly really high and then swoop down and kill smaller birds and mice and things. They can fly at terrific speeds, and their eyes are really sharp; they can see eight or nine times better than people can."

Margaret dropped the tie. "You know a lot about birds, don't you?"

"Not really. I just saw a documentary once on eagles at the cinema and it stuck in my head."

We went on talking till the band leader on stage called the end of the set; then we parted company like all the other couples around us. As soon as the next dance was called, I went back over to where Margaret was sitting and asked her up again. The band broke into a waltz.

I was a little tense putting my arms around her slim waist, but as soon as we started moving down the dance floor I relaxed. Margaret pressed close against me and rested her cheek on my shoulder. There was a smell of flowers from her hair and a minty smell from her breath when she spoke. While I was leading her around the floor, I began to grow more confident. I became good at avoiding collisions with other dancers and managed to make a few graceful swirls on the turns. Every time I pulled off one of these manoeuvres successfully, Margaret smiled. "Now you're getting the knack of it."

When the slow set came to an end, I suggested going to the mineral bar for a lemonade. While we were sipping on our straws at the edge of the dance floor, Hearn went dancing by in front of us. When he spotted me talking to Margaret, he gave me a sly wink. I smiled back at him, proud that he had seen me with such a good-looking girl.

Margaret remained with me for the rest of the dance, then agreed to let me walk her home.

Outside the hall, I plucked up the courage to take her hand. We set off strolling down O'Connell Street. When we reached the traffic lights in the centre of town, I noticed that it was five to eleven by Roches Stores' clock. I remembered my mother's deadline but didn't give it a second thought. My attention was so taken up with Margaret I hardly realised where we were going till we came to St John's Castle. Crossing Thomond Bridge, it began to dawn on me that we were heading into Island Field, an area of town that had a reputation for being a dangerous place to walk in after dark. When we came to the Treaty Stone, Margaret stopped suddenly.

"This is very far out of your way. You needn't come any farther. You'll have a long walk back as it is. I can go the rest of the way by myself."

"No, no. I'll walk you to your door."

Margaret smiled. "The Island has a bad reputation, but the part where I live is very respectable. There's never any trouble there."

I glanced round at a few unfamiliar buildings. "I hardly know this part of town at all. I'll have to follow your lead."

"It's not too far now, just a few streets away."

Margaret's house turned out to be a small semi-detached corporation house with a hedgerow running round the small front garden. Margaret glanced through the gate at one of the front windows, where a chink of light was showing through the curtains. "I can't invite you in, I'm afraid, unless you'd like to meet my mother. She always stays up till I get in. She's a real worrier."

I drew her away from the view of the window into the shadow of the hedge and put my arms around her. We started kissing. Margaret's hand came up and touched my chest, and her tongue suddenly entered my mouth. I stiffened with surprise. I had French-kissed girls in the past, but this was the first time any girl had ever French-kissed me. As her tongue went back and forth in my mouth, her fingers ran up and down over the silky material of my tie, right where the eagle was positioned. I began to feel a light, floating sensation in my head. For a few dizzy moments, I felt like I was rising above myself. I closed my eyes and clung on to Margaret's back. The kiss went on for ages. I began to run out of breath. I tried desperately to keep it going but eventually felt so light-headed I had to break away for air. When I opened my eyes, I drew a deep breath and blinked. I was seeing stars.

Margaret started readjusting her clothes. "I'd better go in now or my mother'll have a canary. Thanks a lot for walking me home. I had a lovely night."

As she walked away, I plucked up the courage to call her back. "How about meeting again some other night? We could go to the pictures or something?"

Margaret hesitated. "I don't think so. I really enjoyed your company, but you're very young."

"No, I'm not. I bet I'm as old as you."

Margaret looked at me. "You must be sixteen so. That's the age I am. Most people think I'm younger because I'm small, but that's how old I am. I swear."

I pretended not to be surprised. "What's age got to do with it, anyway?"

Margaret laughed. "I don't know. I've just never gone out with anyone as young as you before, that's all."

"I'm only asking you to go to the pictures. It's no big deal!"

Margaret bit her lip. "OK, I'll meet you so. Sunday night at seven. Where?"

I thought for a moment. "How about outside Todd's?"

"Fine. I'll see you there at seven. I must go in now or my mother'll be out looking for me. Goodnight."

"Goodnight."

As soon as she was inside her front door, I turned on my heels and started running as fast as I could to try and make it home before midnight. By the time I reached the Treaty Stone, I was out of breath. I stopped in the middle of Thomond Bridge and looked down at the river. The dark water was flowing swiftly at full tide. The sound of the fast current raced in my ears. I thought of my mother and father and wondered how they were going to react to my getting in late; then I reminded myself that I was thirteen. I looked upriver. The lights of Sarsfield Bridge were wavering in the black water. Watching them, I became almost mesmerised. I closed my eyes and thought of the long kiss I'd had with Margaret. I grew light headed thinking of her minty tongue in my mouth, but then I remembered the three year age gap between us and the kiss went out of my head. I shivered. A cold breeze I hadn't noticed till now made me button up my jacket. I started walking slowly towards King John's Castle. The street ahead was dark and dismal. Most of the buildings around the castle were dilapidated. I spat on the pavement and cursed under my breath.

ASHES, SALT AND VINEGAR

John Duhan, they called me, after you
Oh brother, the blessing has been a burden, too
Cast in the shadow of your early death
While you remain inviolate
INVIOLATE

RAY CHARLES WAS singing 'Take these Chains from My Heart' on the café jukebox. All our eyes were focused on a glass in the centre of the Formica table. It contained a thick brownish liquid made up of ashes, salt and vinegar. Hearn turned away from the concoction with a look of disgust. "This is gettin' out of hand, lads. Sugar, salt and coke is one thing, but this is revolting. I'm certainly not going to drink it. Are you, Johnny?"

I raised the glass to my nose, sniffed it and took a sip. "A little too much salt, but not as bad as it looks. Here, Alfredo, have a taste?"

"You must be digesting. We're not all mad. You'd need guts of iron to drink that stuff."

I started to push the glass to the inside of the table, thinking that none of the others were going to try it, but then Garvey (one of the newest members of our gang) put his hand out and took it from me. He looked at it for a moment, took a deep breath and then put the glass to his lips and swallowed the entire contents in a single gulp without gag-ging. The rest of us looked on in amazement. Hearn put his hand to his lips and groaned. "I think I'm going to puke just looking at you. How did you do it?"

Garvey picked up Alfredo's bottle of coke and took a swig. "Simple. Mind over matter. But I wish ye hadn't put so much vinegar in it. I hate vinegar. I don't even have it on chips."

I looked at Garvey. "Do you not feel sick?"

Garvey grinned. "I'll get over it. Anyone got a fag? I think I deserve one after that."

Alfredo took twenty Rothmans from his pocket and offered them round the table. "I can't understand why ye play this game. It's disgusting. What's the point of it?"

I lit my cigarette from Alfredo's match. "It's a question of nerve and guts."

Alfredo sniggered. "I'd hate to have Garvey's guts right now with all that shit floating around in them."

Garvey stared at Alfredo. "We wouldn't expect a wop like you to know anything about guts. It's well known that all Ities are yellow bellies."

Alfredo grinned and looked at his watch. "This wop is going to have to go inside the counter and start dishing up fish and chips soon. People will be coming in from the pictures."

I grabbed Alfredo's wrist and looked at his watch. "Is it that time already? I'm going to have to mosey. Are you coming, Hearn? I don't want to be late for the top twenty on Luxembourg."

Garvey took a pull from his cigarette. "Hang on a minute till I finish this fag and I'll be up part of the way with ye."

"OK, but hurry up. The charts will be started."

Garvey shook his head. "I can't understand why you listen to all that crap in the top twenty, Johnny."

I shrugged. "Ninety-five per cent of it might be crap, but the other five per cent makes the world go round as far as I'm concerned. Listen to Ray Charles there. That was in the top twenty and it's a terrific song."

Alfredo blew smoke down his nose. "Have you heard 'Catch the Wind' by Donovan?"

I sat forward. "It's a nice song, but I don't think it was a good idea putting the word wind in the title. It reminds you straightaway of 'Blowing in the Wind' by Dylan."

Hearn threw his eyes up to the ceiling. "Here he goes again on his hobby-horse about Bob Dylan. Ever since Mary Lee's sister came back from college a few months back and played him *The Freewheelin' Bob Dylan* album, he's been obsessed with the man. Yesterday afternoon he dragged me down to Clancy's record shop and spent nearly an hour and a half in one of the booths listening to his LPs. Most of the songs made no sense to me, but your man here thinks the whole of modern music is going to be changed by what he's doing."

I sat forward. "Bob Dylan is the most important songwriter in the world. There's no one to touch him. Even his love songs are different. They're saying things that no one has ever said in song before. He's going to be huge."

Groups of people started coming into the café. Among them I spotted Margaret. She was coming down the aisle towards our table with a fella in a dark suit. A month or so earlier, I had chickened out of the date I'd made with her because of the age gap between us. As she passed our table, I turned my head towards the wall so she wouldn't see me, but Hearn recognised her. "Hey, Johnny, isn't that the bird you met at the *céilí* a while back? A nice bit of stuff!"

Alfredo grunted. "I wouldn't mind half an hour up a lane with her. What was she like, Johnny?"

"All right." I took a pull from my cigarette and looked towards the door. "I wonder what film all these people are coming from?"

Alfredo blew a smoke ring. "*Rasputin*. It's still on at the Carlton. We saw it last Saturday night, remember? They retained it for another week due to popular demand. It's the orgy scene they all go to see, but there's nothing in it."

Hearn gaped at Alfredo. "What orgy scene? I don't remember any orgy."

I laughed. "Maybe that's 'cause you were too busy trying to have your own orgy with June Flanagan."

Hearn blew smoke in my face. "Not too busy to spot you tryin' to get your paw up Trudy Flynn's skirt."

Alfredo grinned. "You're wasting your time there, Johnny. I tried to drop the hand on her once and she nearly broke my wrist."

43

I smirked. "Would you blame her, after that stunt you pulled on Patsy Miller with the Evostick. You pervert!"

All the boys broke into a fit of laughter. I got to my feet and glanced down the café to where Margaret was sitting. She had her back to me, her long blonde hair flowing around her shoulders. She was laughing at something the fella in the suit was saying.

"Come on, if ye're coming. I'm going to miss the bottom end of the charts as it is."

On our way uptown, Garvey took a harmonica from his pocket and started vamping some blues. Going by Woolworth's, he stopped playing and cleared his throat. "I forgot to tell ye, I read in the paper this morning that the Rolling Stones are coming to the Adelphi in Dublin in a few months' time. I'm thinking of going up to see them. Maybe ye'd come along? We'd need to book well in advance."

Hearn looked at Garvey. "If it was the Beatles I'd hop at it, but the Stones! Still, it would be gas making the trip. I'm sure Alf would go. Maybe Fraser, too."

Garvey put his harmonica in his pocket. "We'd have to stay overnight in a B&B. What do you think, Johnny?"

"I don't think I'd be allowed go, but I'll ask."

Garvey parted company from us at Cecil Street. Hearn and myself continued on up O'Connell Avenue. When we arrived at Wolfe Tone Street, I left Hearn and ran on ahead. My father answered our front door.

"I thought you were told to be in by ten o'clock! Your brothers and sisters are all in bed. You have school tomorrow, remember!"

"Sorry, Dad, I lost track of the time. Where's Mam?"

"She went to bed when we got in from the pub. She's not feeling well."

I followed my father into the living room. He sat in his old armchair by the fire and picked up a large white copy of the Bible. Frank Sinatra's smooth voice was coming through the open hatch from a radio in the kitchen singing 'Strangers in the Night'.

"Do you mind if I change stations, Dad?"

"Fire away. But pull back the sliding glass so I don't have to listen to the noise."

In the kitchen I closed the glass hatch and went over to the mahogany radio on the delph cabinet and started tuning the dial. A garble of foreign voices and snatches of foreign songs crackled in and out of frequency as the white arrow shot down through the row of stations. When it reached Luxembourg, 'My Generation' by The Who came fizzling through the copper speaker grill at low volume. I yanked the control knob up a few notches and pulled up a chair. Out in the living room my father hopped up and glared at me through the glass hatch. I turned the volume down a little and smiled back at him.

After 'My Generation' ended, the DJ's high-pitched voice came on the air and announced that we were now entering the top ten best-selling records in Great Britain. "Stay tuned, folks, and we'll be right back after these commercials with a bright new entry by the Swinging Blue Jeans. . ."

Though most of the songs in the top ten turned out to be mediocre, I kept my ear glued to the speaker for the next half hour. When the charts ended, I tuned the radio back to BBC and returned to the living room.

"Still reading the Bible, Dad?" I went and stood by the fireplace and warmed my hands from the dying coals.

My father looked at me over the rims of his reading glasses. "I have most of it read. It's a puzzling book, full of wild contradictions. The Old Testament is all vengeance, blood and guts, and the New Testament turns the whole thing on its head and talks about turning the other cheek. Each of the Gospels has different accounts of the same events. Matthew spends pages giving you Joseph's family tree going back to King David, even though Joseph is supposed to have had nothing to do with the virgin birth. And the descriptions of the resurrection are different in each of the Gospels. It's baffling. But then I never believed in the virgin birth or the resurrection to begin with. As far as I'm concerned, when you die that's the end of you. They put you down a hole, and you're gone for ever."

"Mam doesn't believe that."

"I know, son. She believes in all the pie in the sky stuff. She's a dreamer."

"I think I believe in it too, Dad."

My father smiled. "You're a dreamer too, son, like your mother. I was always a doubting Thomas myself. That's my nature."

"Then why are you reading the Bible?"

My father shrugged. "Curiosity."

I was feeling tired, but it wasn't often that my father opened up to me like this, so I remained by the fire pretending I was heating my hands. After a short silence I cleared my throat. "I hope Mam doesn't have to go back into hospital again."

My father looked up from the Bible. "I hope so, too. But she's been a bit low in herself again lately. If she does go in, it won't be for long, just a few weeks. They might need to do some checks on her to see if she's on the right medication."

"Why does it keep happening to her, Dad?"

My father hesitated. "I don't know, son. I think it goes back to when she was young. Her mother died when she was only four; then her father took to the drink and she and her two sisters were orphaned out to different relatives. I'm sure that had a big effect on her. But you knew about that, didn't you?"

I nodded. "Joan told me before she went to live in England. But how come Mam's two sisters stayed OK?"

"I guess they were stronger than she was."

I could tell by the stiff look on his face that my father was uneasy with this subject, but there were things I had always wanted to ask him about my mother. "Joan also told me that Mam had her first breakdown after your first son died, before I was born. I always found it strange that you named me after him. I'll never forget the shock I got when I discovered his death certificate in the old tin box you keep your documents in upstairs. He died of some kind of a fever, didn't he?"

My father took a deep breath. "Gastroenteritis. I was called back from sea when it happened. My own father who lived here in the house with us at the time died on the same day the child died. The two of them were buried together. Your mother had nursed both of them for months, so she was very run down. The sight of the little white coffin on top of the big one was heartbreaking. Your mother held up well enough on the day of the funeral, though she didn't actually go to the service as it was the custom in those days for mothers not to attend the burial of their first son. But two weeks after the funeral we had to take her to St Joseph's. They kept her there for almost three months. In the end, I had to threaten the psychiatrist that, if he didn't let her out, I was going to break into the place and free her myself. He discharged her the day after that. The whole thing was a terrible strain on all of us. But life goes on. You have to be strong and accept these things when they happen or else you buckle up and go under. The Bible here is full of such tragedies. Job in particular. His whole family was wiped out and he still kept going."

My father picked up the poker and started jabbing at the cinders. "Life is tough for everyone, son. You'll learn that as you grow up. That prayer your mother is always saying, the *Salve Regina*, sums up this world accurately enough where it calls it a valley of tears."

I stood in silence looking down at the ashes around the grate for a few moments; then I said goodnight to my father and went upstairs.

My three brothers were asleep in our room, so I didn't turn on the light. In bed I automatically started saying my prayers. Halfway through my first Hail Mary, the faint sound of my mother coughing in the room next door distracted me. The words my father had used to describe what had become of her and her sisters when their mother died came into my head: "orphaned out". While I was thinking of this, an old memory came back to me of a visit I'd made with my mother many years before to a quiet old couple who lived in a small, dark house in a lane in a run-down part of the city. The woman, whom my mother called "Nanna", was blind and her husband, who spoke very little, had a long white beard. Thinking back on it now, I realised that this bleak house was where my mother had grown up. I shivered at the thought and turned in the bed.

My dead brother John came into my thoughts. I pictured his small coffin lying on top of my grandfather's coffin and my mother in tears beside it. I imagined the terrible fear she must have felt at the thought of being left in a house where my father was absent most of the time. St Joseph's, where she was taken after her breakdown, came into my head. The grim grey building was overshadowed in my memory by the high barbed wired walls of the city jail. While I was trying to imagine what it must have been like for her being locked up there on that first occasion, the terrible realisation dawned on me that the cemetery where my brother John was buried was just up the street from St Joseph's.

My father's footsteps coming upstairs interrupted my train of thought. I listened to him entering his and my mother's bedroom. I started thinking about his part in the tragedy. I tried to imagine how he must have felt coming home and finding his father and son dead and his wife on the verge of a nervous breakdown. The thought of it made me shake in the bed. Tears started pouring from my eyes. I buried my face in the pillow to dampen the sound of my sobbing.

The wheezing sound of my brothers sleeping in the bunks opposite me drew my attention. They were fast asleep. As far as I knew, none of them were aware that they had a dead brother. But, sharing his name, I could almost feel his absence lying in the bed beside me.

ROLLING STONES

One hundred miles from his home
Through a lonely city he roams
Till he finds a bed for his tired bones
In a house for rolling stones
ONE HUNDRED MILES

ARVEY AND MYSELF arrived at St Vincent de Paul's night shelter just after one o'clock in the morning, having been told about the place by a passer-by who had come upon us lying on the pavement a few blocks away. An old attendant answered the door and invited us into the hall. Another attendant – a slightly younger man – came along and gave us a hard look. "Surely you're not looking for a bed for the night? Where are you from and what are you doing out so late? Won't your parents be worried about you?"

Garvey showed no sign of answering the man, so I cleared my throat. "We're from down the country, sir. We came to Dublin this morning with a few friends for the Rolling Stones' concert at the Adelphi. During the day we lost our money, so we couldn't afford a place to stay. A man we met in the street gave us your address and told us you might put us up for the night."

The attendants looked at one another; then the younger of the two started shaking his head. "This hostel is for older men, men in poor circumstances. What age are you?"

"Fifteen, sir. We're both fifteen." I didn't blink an eye adding a year to my age.

The older attendant looked at us sympathetically, then turned to the other man. "We'll have to take them in, Pat. It's nearly a quarter past one. Where are they going to go at this hour if we don't take them?"

"I suppose you're right, Jack. We'd better get them to sign their names and addresses in the ledger before you take them up. Come over here, boys, and write your names and addresses in this book."

While we were following the attendant to a desk in a corner of the hallway, I congratulated myself on having lied so convincingly to the two old men. The real reason we hadn't been able to afford a B&B was that we had spent most of the money our parents had given us on clothes – Garvey on a purple shirt with elephant collars and I on a red and green pair of plaid hipsters. Hearn and Alfredo had tried to stop us from buying the clothes, but Garvey and myself thought that it would be no bother roughing it on the streets for one night. Two fearful hours of traipsing the unfamiliar city in the dark had been more than enough to show us the error of our ways.

I decided to use a false name and address so that my parents couldn't be informed of our stay in the hostel. While I was writing in the ledger, the doorbell rang. The older attendant went to answer it and came back a few moments later with a bearded tramp weighed down with plastic carrier bags. The younger attendant smiled familiarly at the newcomer. "You're late tonight, Seamus. Out on a spree, were you? You may as well go straight up with these two lads as soon as they're ready, and Jack'll fix you up in your usual place."

I handed Garvey the biro and gave him a wink to indicate that he should follow my example and write a false name and address in the book. He got the message.

We followed the old attendant up a high flight of stairs. Near the top I stood back to let the tramp go before me and accidentally knocked one of the plastic bags out of his hand. When it hit the step, hundreds of cigarette butts spilled out all over the stairway. Immediately the tramp bent down and started picking them up. I was just about to bend down to help him, but the attendant stopped me. "Leave that! I'll do it later when you're asleep. Come on now, Seamus, it's very late. We need to get these boys to bed."

We followed the attendant down a dimly lit corridor. On the way we ran into an old man in rags carrying a small enamel saucepan. As we passed him, I glanced into the pot and saw a fish head and a few bones floating around in some greasy liquid. I shuddered and walked on.

Near the end of the corridor, the attendant showed Garvey and myself into a large dormitory divided into a dozen or more walled-off cubicles. He appointed us two of these adjoining one another near the door. "You'll be fine here, boys. I'll leave the door slightly ajar so that you'll have some light to get undressed by. There'll be another attendant on duty in the morning who'll look after you when you get up. Goodnight now."

After the attendant left, I started sniffing the air. "This place would give you the willies, wouldn't it? Do you get the smell? It's like dead bodies or something."

Garvey pulled a long face. "It smells like stale piss to me."

I looked down the dormitory at the row of cubicles which were just about visible in the dim light coming in from the corridor. "At least we have a roof over our heads."

Garvey rubbed his eyes and yawned. "I'm shagged after all the walking. Let's go to bed."

"See you in the morning."

Garvey grinned. "Hopefully."

My cubicle contained a single iron bed and a small wooden locker. The dividing walls between the cubicles were thin and didn't go all the way to the ceiling. Coughing and wheezing noises could be heard coming from every quarter of the room. I undressed and got under the coarse sheets and rough blankets. There was a damp, musty smell from my pillow, so I put my shirt over it. Then I said a few quick prayers and tried to settle down for the night. Though I was exhausted I found it hard to sleep. Somewhere in the dormitory, someone started coughing, a loud, dry, barking cough that went on for ages. My mother and father came into my head. I remembered the assurances I had given them that I would act responsibly during the trip. I looked around the dark cubicle and wondered what they would say if they could see me now.

51

The coughing in the room went on and on. After tossing and turning for over an hour, I finally managed to nod off.

A bell woke me early next morning. I hopped out of bed, got dressed and went next door to Garvey's cubicle. Garvey was sitting on the edge of his bed putting on his shoes. When he saw me he shook his head. "What a night! I didn't sleep a wink with all those tossers coughing and snorting. How about you?"

"I had a bad night, too, but it's over now. Grab your bag and let's go."

Outside the dormitory we followed a group of down-and-outs to a washroom at the end of the corridor. There were rows of sinks on either side of the narrow room with wide mirrors above them. Garvey and I started throwing water on our faces. On either side of us, men stripped to the waist were shaving and washing, some of them chatting and joking while lathering their faces. One man in a dirty grey vest looked down at Garvey's pointed shoes and started laughing. "Janey Mac, will you look at the pointy toes on them things! You wouldn't get far on a football field with them yokes on you."

Garvey smiled but kept his mouth shut.

After our wash, we went downstairs and found a new attendant on duty, a much younger man than the attendants we'd dealt with the night before. I thanked him for putting us up for the night and told him we were leaving. He looked us up and down and smiled. "You must be Frank and Joe? Jack told me about you before he went off duty earlier this morning. He said to make sure you got a good breakfast before you left. If you don't mind waiting till after eight o'clock mass, we'll give you a good feed, and then you can go on your way. The waiting room's just down the corridor there, on your left."

We thanked the attendant and walked off down the narrow hall. When we got out of earshot, Garvey turned to me and sniggered. "How're you keeping, Frank?"

"Not bad, Joe. How's youself?"

The waiting room was full of men dressed in shabby clothes, some with tattered suitcases by their chairs, others holding carrier-bags in their laps. A few of them were talking quietly. Most were silent.

Garvey and myself found a few free chairs near the door. I looked at a few of the men sitting around us. Their faces were grey and careworn.

I had seen down-and-outs in the past but never so many all grouped together in one place. I began to feel a sense of weariness looking at them.

Garvey gave me a nudge and looked across the room. A young man with a tight crew-cut and bulging eyes was staring at us. When he noticed us looking at him, he got up from his chair and came over and took the seat right beside me. His head was bobbing up and down continuously. He muttered something to himself and then turned his head towards me without looking directly into my eyes.

"You're new here, aren't you?"

I hesitated. "Yes."

"I knew by your clothes." He turned away from me and looked around the room, his head bobbing up and down all the time. After another few moments, he cleared his throat and started to tell me in a half whisper, without batting an eyelid, that his name was Jesus Christ. "No one here believes me, but, I swear, that's who I am."

I held back a smile and looked into his face. His eyes were all red and bloodshot, as though he had been crying. He had a twitch at the corner of his mouth and his chin was spiked with stubble. I didn't know what to say to him, so I just nodded and looked away. A man sitting opposite me winked and put his finger to his temple and twisted it. A few moments later, the attendant came into the room and announced that it was time for mass.

Garvey and myself took a pew near the back of the small chapel. I knelt and said a prayer. Garvey sat beside me picking at his nails.

When the priest arrived on the altar, I followed the service devoutly, as did most of the down-and-outs around us. Halfway through the mass – just as the priest was about to perform the Eucharist – Garvey gave me a nudge and threw his eyes up towards the altar. I ignored him at first, but then I heard some commotion going on at the front of the chapel, so I looked up. The man with the crew-cut was standing by the altar rails with his hands raised above his chin as though he was about to bless the congregation. The priest lowered the host and asked for some volunteers to come to his assistance. A couple of down-and-outs rushed over and led the disturbed man down the aisle towards the door. Garvey looked at me and threw his eyes up to the ceiling. The priest went on with the service.

After mass, we followed the crowd leaving the church to a large dining room, where we were given a full fried breakfast. Not having eaten since before the concert the evening before, we devoured everything on our plates. After the meal, we thanked the attendant again and left the building.

Out in the early morning streets, Garvey took a deep breath. "That's one night I'll never forget as long as I live."

I laughed. "Wait till we tell Hearn and the boys about it. They'll never believe us."

We walked on in silence for a few moments. Garvey kicked a pebble off the pavement. "I was just thinking about the concert last night. It seems a lifetime away now, doesn't it?"

I laughed. "Yeah. The Stones were great, though, weren't they?"

Garvey spat in the gutter. "They were good all right, but not as good as real blues singers like Leadbelly and Howling Wolf. I have lots of blues records at home. I must play them for you sometime."

"I'd like to hear them."

Garvey kicked another pebble. "I've been thinking of starting a rhythm 'n' blues band myself for some time. I know a couple of guitarists. And Alfredo is always talking about getting a kit of drums. I'd play the harmonica myself and do a bit of singing. You could be the main singer, if you like?"

"Who, me?"

Garvey smiled. "Why not? Everyone knows you have a good voice. Alfredo was telling me you won a talent contest one time. Is that right?"

I shrugged. "Hearn sang with me. And we came second, not first."

Garvey looked at me. "Alfredo said you stole the show."

I laughed. "You should have seen the opposition: a bowlegged tap-dancer, a ventriloquist with a stutter and a fat woman who sang 'Danny Boy' in a wobbly falsetto. She scooped first prize. By right, we should have got it, but our parish priest objected to the song we sang, Rave On."

"The bollix."

"He was an old man."

Garvey put his arm around my shoulder. "Well, are you on for it?"

"What, starting a band? I'll think about it."

THE INTENTIONS

With the courthouse supplying the rules
And hospitals searching for cures
ALWAYS REMEMBER

WHEN I ARRIVED at the Regional Hospital, I found Garvey in good spirits, despite the fact that he had been laid up for two days with a broken collar bone and other injuries, having been involved in an accident a couple of nights earlier in a stolen car. As I approached his bed in the public ward, he put his hand to his mouth to stop himself from smiling.

"Don't make me laugh whatever you do. It hurts even when I smile. Where did you hear about me?"

I noticed a number of cuts and bruises on the left side of his face as I sat down beside the bed. "Hearn heard about it from Fraser last night in Orlando's, and he told me about it this morning on the way to school. I couldn't believe it. You're an awful eejit. Why'd you do it?"

Garvey shrugged. "You know me: I'm a sucker for fast cars. Funny thing is, I was only going seventy when I hit the wall. I was doing a ton before that. A squad was on my tail. It nearly went up my arse. The two fellows with me – you don't know them – got out with minor cuts and bruises, but

I broke my collar bone and injured my right knee. I might have got away only for that."

I shook my head. "What'll happen to you now, do you think?"

Garvey widened his eyes and laughed. "Probably be sent down for ten years. I'll really be able to play the blues then. Can you see me blowing my harp in a nine by six cell for twelve hours a day. I'll really get the tone right there."

I looked into his swollen eyes, stuck for words. The fact that he had mentioned his harmonica made me feel awkward. Five or six months earlier, we had started a rhythm 'n' blues group together. After our first live performance – a support spot for a showband at a local dance hall – Garvey overheard someone criticising his voice and harmonica playing and left the band soon after.

"You still play the harmonica, do you?"

"I just play along with records now. Leadbelly, Muddy Waters, Sonny Terry and Brownie McGee, the same ones we listened to together when you used to call to my house."

I shifted uneasily in my chair, remembering a time when I used to visit Garvey's house almost every day after school to listen to his blues records. His father was dead and his mother worked as an office cleaner down-town, so he had a free house most afternoons. I had enjoyed going there for the music and chat, but his house had always seemed very bleak and empty. Despite the fact that it was spotlessly clean, it had an atmosphere of being only half lived in. Often when I left there in the evenings to return to the hustle and bustle of my own home, I felt sorry for Garvey, thinking of him alone in his empty living room surrounded by family photographs and shiny ornaments.

"How's your mother taking this? It must be tough on her."

Garvey shifted in the bed. "She'll be all right. My brother Mike'll look after her. He came out to see me yesterday evening. Missed his football practice over it. He ate the head off me. But he's going to get me a good solicitor."

Garvey's older brother Mike was married with a young kid. He man-aged a shoe shop in town and coached a soccer team in his spare time.

"Well, at least you'll have that. And you'll need it. This is really serious business you're after getting yourself into."

Garvey shrugged and changed the subject: "How're things at school?"

"The usual. Preparing for the finals. If I pass them, my father has a job lined up for me as an apprentice turner."

"A good job."

"Before I was expelled from the Christian Brothers, I used to dream of being an architect."

Garvey took a deep breath. "I was hoping to become a mechanic myself, but I don't know what'll happen now."

"Maybe you'll get off."

"Maybe."

We sat in silence for a few moments. I took a cheap bar of Turkish Delight from my jacket pocket and threw it on the bed. Garvey picked it up and smiled. "My favourite! How did you remember?"

"It was all I could afford." I turned away and looked around the ward. There were just three other beds in the room. In one there was a middle-aged man with plaster of Paris on one arm; in another a patient in bright yellow pyjamas was reading a newspaper; and in the third a young man was sleeping. On the lockers beside each of the beds, there were bottles of Lucozade and lemonade and bowls of fruit and get-well cards. Below a crucifix at the end of the ward, a TV set was glowing at low volume.

I turned back to Garvey. "It must be boring for you here, but at least you have the telly."

Garvey glanced at the TV set dismissively. "Are you not going to tell me about how the band's been doing? I hear you've made a few changes since I left."

I was expecting this question to pop up, but it still threw me off balance. "We're doing OK. It's a totally different band. We've even changed the name. We're called The Intentions now. Joe is gone. Billy is still on bass, and a fella called Johnny McMahon – or Mac, as we call him – is playing lead guitar. Alfredo's got a new kit of drums and manages to get through a full song now without dropping a beat. Oh, yeah, and Hearn also joined us as a second singer soon after you left. But you knew that, didn't you?"

Garvey frowned. "I heard about it all right but I couldn't believe it! That little bollix isn't much better than me at singing. How did ye come to take him on?"

"We got a request for him to sing at one of our gigs, and then someone suggested that he join. That was over a month ago now."

Garvey sneered. "Who sent up the request; himself, was it?"

I couldn't recall who had suggested that Hearn sing with us, but I did remember putting in a good word for him when his name came up to join the band, though I didn't want to tell Garvey this as I knew it would be a sore point with him after the way he had felt obliged to leave the band himself.

"We needed a good backing singer. We've been doing a few soul and Motown songs in our set recently. You need lots of backing vocals for them."

Garvey frowned. "You should stick to rhythm 'n' blues. It's more authentic."

"I don't know about that. Otis Redding and Marvin Gaye are great singers, and Smokey Robinson and The Miracles have the purest voices I know."

Garvey raised his head. "Yeah, but it's all a bit stagey, don't you think?"

"Some of it, not all."

An old nurse came along and stuck a thermometer in Garvey's mouth and started strapping his arm up for a blood test. I had a band rehearsal to attend – something I didn't want to mention to Garvey – so I took the opportunity to take my leave. I rose from the chair and touched his arm. "I'd better go. I'll try and stay in touch in the future. It was good seeing you again. And the best of luck with the you-know-what when it comes up. I'll be keeping an eye out to see how you get on."

The thermometer was still in Garvey's mouth. He raised his free hand as a parting gesture. When I reached the door, I looked back and smiled.

Outside the hospital I thought of catching a bus into town but decided to walk the two miles instead. I had thought that this visit to see Garvey might have eased my conscience for having neglected to stay in contact with him since he'd left the band, but, if anything, I felt even worse now. I quickened my pace to try and shake off the bad feeling.

I came to the Pike, a small river with a bridge going over it, a place where I had played and fished as a small boy many years before. I stopped in the middle of the bridge and looked upstream to a spot where I'd once floated on a raft made from a few beams of wood tied together. Hearn had been with me at the time, but he had been too scared to go out on the raft. As I remembered this now, I found myself thinking that, had Garvey been with me then, he not only would have accompanied me out on the raft but would probably have danced on it in the middle of the river, to heighten the thrill.

During the rest of the long walk back to town, Garvey never left my mind. By the time I arrived in the city centre, I was running late for the band rehearsal, so I went straight to our practice hall. When I got there, I found that the boys had the musical equipment set up on stage ready to go. The first thing that caught my eye when I walked into the hall was the band's new name printed in bold black capitals on the front of Alfredo's bass drum: **THE INTENTIONS**.

Alfredo was the first to notice my arrival. As I walked towards the stage, he got up from his drum stool and looked out over his cymbals. "About time, Johnny. What kept you?"

"I went out to the Regional after tea to see Garvey."

The band's bass player, Billy, stopped tuning his instrument and looked down at me. "How's he doing? Hearn told us about the crash. Is he in bad shape?"

"Considering he hit a wall at seventy miles an hour, he's not bad at all. He's cut and bruised and has a broken collar bone, but he's in good spirits. He was asking for you all, by the way."

Hearn glanced at me from the back of the stage. "The poor bastard. He'll go down for this. He has a record, you know. Fraser reckons he'll get six months at least. Maybe more."

There was a long silence. I hopped up on the stage beside Mac at one of the backing microphones and turned to Hearn. "Well, let's get on with it. If you want to try that new song by Wilson Picket, go ahead. I'll back you up, this time."

THE FOUNDRY

Surrounded by factories and prisons
ALWAYS REMEMBER

I WAS FILING a flat piece of metal when Peader came along and placed a heavy steel rod in the vice beside the one I was working on. When he had it clamped between the gripping jaws, he turned to me and smiled. "Well, chief, how's it goin' today? No accidents so far, I hope?"

I took a quick look down towards the foreman's glass-panelled office in the centre of the shop floor. "Not so far. I've been filing these blasted steel plates all morning. I have a pain in my wrist from it. After yesterday's cock-up on the lathe, the boss probably doesn't want to risk putting me on another machine for a while."

The previous day, the foreman had given me my first chance to operate a lathe, and I'd made a complete mess of the job and buckled the tool holder. After assessing the damage, the foreman had called me a "dunder-head" and offered the opinion that I wasn't suited to the work.

Peader laughed. "Don't worry, chief, you'll get the hang of it in time. You just need to lose your fear of the machines, that's all. It's a bit like my scuba-diving. The first time I went down, I was terrified – I could barely swim at the time – but now you can't keep me away from the sea. Did I tell you, we were off again last weekend, up near the Cliffs of Moher? It was terrific. It's another world down there. Everything goes into slow motion once you go below the surface. It's hard to explain, but I feel really at home under the sea. I'd swap places with the fish any day. We're going off again next weekend, further up the coast. I'm really looking forward to it."

I looked at Peader. His natural red complexion had grown an even deeper shade of red from the excitement of talking about his favourite hobby. Since I had started working at the foundry a few weeks earlier, he had been like a brother to me. He kept his eye out for me at all times to make sure that I wasn't getting into difficulty, and whenever I messed up a job, he consoled me with stories of bigger mishaps that he himself had had when he first came to work in the turning room a few years before.

Though he had already told me about his weekend's diving experiences a couple of days earlier, I gave him my full attention again, knowing how much it meant to him.

"I don't know how you do it, Peader. What would you do if your oxygen pump got cut on a reef at the bottom of the sea? Would you not be worried that you might run out of air before you reached the surface?"

Peader laughed. "You've been watching too much TV, chief. That never happens. But last summer one of the divers in our team got into difficulty when his watch stopped without him realising it while we were on the ocean floor. He ran out of air and was nearly unconscious by the time we got him to the surface, but we managed to revive him easy enough. We never go down very deep. You'd need to go way out to sea for that. . ."

Our conversation was interrupted by a prolonged blast of a siren. Within the space of a few seconds, the foundry went completely silent as machine after machine was knocked off for the one o'clock lunch break.

I followed Peader and some other workers to a row of lockers and got my lunch bag; then I made my way to the iron stove at the front of the foreman's office, where already groups of turners and apprentice turners were assembled, sitting around on stools and other objects on the floor. One of the workers had made a pot of tea, which was sitting on top of the stove. I got in line and filled my mug; then I went and sat beside Peader on some upturned iron flanges.

While we were chewing our sandwiches, a couple of the senior apprentices sitting close by started talking about a football match that one of them had attended the evening before in the Market's Field. Other members of the workforce joined in the conversation, and soon the debate became quite lively. Peader tried to chip in with a comment on goalkeeping, but one of the older apprentices gave him a sour look. "What the fuck would you know about it, Peader? You know nothing about football. Stick to your snorkels and flippers! When we want your opinion, we'll ask for it."

Peader went silent but didn't appear too upset by the insult. He was used to this kind of treatment from the older apprentices.

After I finished my sandwich, I took a packet of cigarettes from the pocket of my overalls and lit one. Peader looked at me disapprovingly. "You'd think you'd have more respect for your lungs, chief. And you a singer with a band. By the way, have you any more performances coming up. I'd love to go and see you in action some night. The next time ye're playing in the Jetland, let me know, and I'll go along and see if your intentions are good. It must be terrific having all them lovely dolly-birds at your feet."

"Dolly-birds?!"

Peader whistled and drew the shape of a female waistline with the curve of his hands. "You know what I mean, chief. Don't play the innocent. That's probably why you joined a band in the first place, for the dollies. Admit it, go on."

"If it was, Peader, I haven't been very lucky so far."

Peader gave me a sly wink. "Go on, chief. You're a good-looking fella. And we all know what bands get up to after they come off stage. It must be very exciting being with a different dolly every night?"

While Peader was probing me for hot gossip, I looked across the shop floor at one of the oldest members of the workforce, a tall, grey-haired man sitting behind a small lathe which he never left from one end of the day to the other. Having finished his lunch, he was already making adjustments to his machine in preparation for getting back to work. His long, lean fingers were moving around the wheels and pulleys as though he was tuning up a delicate musical instrument. I watched him with incomprehension, puzzled to know how anyone could feel such enthusiasm for a machine.

The siren started blowing. One by one, the motors of the machines started up, and soon the whole foundry was vibrating under its usual loud, iron drone.

Before getting back to work, I went to the toilets out in the main part of the foundry. On my way back to the turning room, I stood for a moment and looked around the plant where dozens of workers were back in full production, hammering, grinding, pounding and welding. Showers of sparks were flying up in bright fountains in every corner of the shop floor. A young apprentice welder with a face mask in his hand came up and made a friendly gesture. "Do you not recognise me? We started working here together on the same day a couple of weeks back. I met you in the head office. We were sitting together, remember?"

I looked at the fella's grimy face. "Oh, yeah, I didn't recognise you there for a minute. How's it going?"

"Great! They haven't let me use the blowtorch yet, but I'm really look-ing forward to it. What's it like in the turning room?"

I pulled a long face. "To be quite honest, I'm not mad about the place. There are no windows in there. No natural light, just electric light. And the noise is deafening."

The apprentice gave me a crooked look. "What are you saying! That's a great job you have. I wanted to become a turner myself, but I couldn't get in because I failed the Group Cert exam. You should count yourself lucky."

I hunched my shoulders and looked around the foundry. "Maybe. But can you imagine spending your entire life in a place like this?! I get the willies just thinking about it."

"What's wrong with it?"

I looked at the fella's puzzled face and realised we were on different planets regarding the foundry. "I'd better get back to the turning room. The boss inside is an awful stickler about time keeping. See you around."

Back at the workbench, I found Peader examining one of the steel plates I'd filed down earlier.

"Not bad, chief, but you might try and keep your hand straight when you're going backwards and forwards with the file. You seem to be dipping a bit at the back. Here, I'll show you how to do it."

While Peader was giving me a demonstration on how to use a file prop-erly, the foreman came up behind me unexpectedly and cleared his throat. "Duhan, you're wanted at head office straightaway. You're needed at home. Your mother's not well, I believe. You'll get the details at the office from whoever brought the news. They're waiting for you out there now. You can leave your file there on the bench. Peader will take it back to the store room if you don't come back."

Though my mother hadn't shown any recent signs of depression, I immediately thought the worst. Without washing my hands or getting out of my overalls, I rushed out to the head office at the front of the building. Surprisingly, Hearn turned out to be the messenger. He was waiting for me by one of the secretaries' desks with a blank look on his face. Beside him one of the bosses of the plant, Mr Foley, offered me some sympathy and told me to take the rest of the afternoon off.

Outside the front gate, Hearn looked me up and down and started laughing at my oily overalls and grimy hobnailed boots. "Christ, look at the state of you! You're mankey. And take a look at them winkle-pickers! Wait till I tell the lads; they'll have a great laugh."

"What's up with my mother, Hearn? How come you learned she was sick?"

Hearn grinned. "Sick my arse! There's nothing wrong with your mother. I just made that up to get you off work. We've had an offer to play a gig in the Go Go Club in Cork tonight. Some Dublin group cancelled out at the last minute, and a call came through to Orlando's asking us if we could fill in for them. Alfredo and myself have spent the last few hours contacting the boys and organising transport. We have to be at the club before seven this evening to set up the equipment. It's a long journey. The van's hired, but the gear has yet to be packed away, so let's get a move on. You can't go to our first important out-of-town gig dressed like that."

THE GO GO

I'm Don Quixote, I'm on the road again
My band's called Sancho, we're on the move again
My horsepower now is in a transit van
DON QUIXOTE

SOMEWHERE OUT IN the dark, smoky, neon-lit club, a harsh voice yelled up in a thick Dublin accent: "Ger off the stage and go back to the bleedin' bog where yous belong, you shower of culchies!"

Two or three other hecklers joined in in abusing us, and soon the sweaty crowd at the front of the stage began to grow uneasy. Eventually the disturbance made it impossible for me to concentrate on the words I was singing. I stopped the band in the middle of Junior Walker's 'Road Runner' and glared out over the sea of heads to try and locate the troublemakers. "Come on, step out of the shadows and let's see your faces, you pack of cowards!"

Hearn came up behind me and pulled me away from the microphone. "For Christ sake, Johnny! Do you not realise where we are?!"

Unlike its sister club in Cork – where we'd had a number of successful gigs over the past few months – the Dublin Go Go attracted some very rough elements. This was our second gig in the place, and because our first spot here had received a favourable mention in Pat Egan's popular rock column in *Spotlight* magazine, a large crowd had turned out to see us. Up until this disturbance, our programme of R&B, soul and Motown music, coupled with our new Detroit image of double-breasted pin-striped suits and trilby hats, had been going down a storm with the crowd.

We played another song and took an early break in the hope that things might settle down in the second half of the show.

During the interval, I took a trip down to the mineral bar at the back of the club to get a coke. While I was returning to the dressing room, some-one grabbed my arm from behind and twisted it halfway up my back. "OK fuckface, we're out of the shadows now. So whar are you goin' to do abour it?"

Two bulldog faces were glaring at me, one on either side. I couldn't see the fella behind me, but from the harsh tone of his voice I could imagine that he was even meaner looking that his friends. He jerked my elbow and told me to start walking slowly towards the exit door. "And don't get any ideas about trying to scarper or I'll bleedin' break your arm!"

"Where are you taking me?"

The fella on my right put his mouth to my ear and laughed. "Up to the Liffey. We're going to fuck you in by the balls! Now keep movin', prick-face, or we'll do you right here!"

As I was being steered towards the exit door, I glanced around the club for a familiar face that might notice the fix I was in, but it was too dark to recognise anybody. We went right by the stage and came to the dressing room. For a moment I thought of calling out Hearn's name, but the record playing in the background was so loud I knew I wouldn't be heard. I walked on, trembling in my boots.

When we came to the exit door, we were stopped by two bouncers who asked if we intended returning to the club. The fella wedging me in on my right smiled at the two men and told them we wouldn't be com-ing back. "We have some unfinished business to see to uptown, haven't we, lads?"

The fella behind me gave my elbow a sudden jerk to warn me not to open my mouth. A dart of pain shot through my arm. I gritted my teeth and my mouth clamped shut. I desperately tried to make eye contact with the bouncers as I was being shunted past them, but it was so dark neither of them saw the fix I was in. One of my captors pushed open the door in front of me and waited for me to step ahead of him. At that moment a sudden wave of fear ran through me and stopped me in my tracks. Instead of going forward, I instinctively took a step back and made a quick struggle to get free of the fella gripping my arm. He wrenched my elbow upwards. I cried out in pain, and immediately the bouncers realised that something was up. One of them lunged at the fella behind me and pinned him to the wall. The other bouncer grabbed the fella on my right by the scruff of the neck, while the third ruffian escaped out the door. After a brief tussle, the bouncers overpowered the two remaining troublemakers and threw them out of the club with a stern warning that they weren't to show their faces inside the door ever again.

After thanking the bouncers, I made my way back to the dressing room, nursing my arm as I went. The band were just getting ready to return to the stage. When I told them of the lucky escape I'd had, Hearn laughed. "That'll teach you not to go spouting your mouth off on stage. You're lucky they didn't cut the balls off you."

The second half of the gig went without a hitch. At the end of the night, the crowd wouldn't let us off stage till we gave them two encores.

As often happened after our gigs, a number of people came to our dressing room door to congratulate us on our performance. Among the well-wishers on this occasion, a fella with strawberry-blonde hair, dressed in a neat gabardine overcoat, stepped forward. "Great show, lads. I love your image. I work in advertising myself, so I know a good thing when I see it. I have a proposition to put to you which you might be interested in. The name's Briggs, Mike Briggs. Can we talk?"

Briggs stepped into the tiny dressing room and offered a packet of Dunhill cigarettes around, placing them in my direction first. "I liked the way you handled that tricky situation in the first half. It could have gone either way there. You needed to assert yourself, and it worked. You really got the crowd behind you."

Hearn laughed. "He got more than the crowd behind him, didn't you, Johnny?"

I looked at Hearn. "Never mind that."

Briggs took a pull from his cigarette and glanced around the grubby dressing room. "The boss of the club was telling me you don't have a manager. For a band as good as yours, this surprised me. Though I'm currently working in advertising, as I said, I've been considering getting into band management for some time. After you hear me out, I'm hoping you might be willing to consider me for the job. This isn't a snap decision on my part. I was at your last performance here a few weeks ago, and I thought you were terrific. For a bunch of country boys, you're way ahead of the posse in your style and sound. You're the first group I've seen around the city with real international potential, and that's what interests me. I assume from your professionalism that your sights are set on overseas markets as well as here?"

Hearn glanced at me, then turned to Briggs. "We have ambitions all right, but we're semi-pro at the moment. We couldn't afford to turn full-time on what we earn."

Briggs blew some smoke towards the ceiling. "I meant long-term aims. But even in the immediate future, I think I could improve your situation. For starters, I'd be able to negotiate better fees for you in places like this. The boss here was telling me the flat rate he pays his bands, but after tonight's performance, your drawing power is sure to improve. This should be reflected in what you're paid."

Mac nodded. "Good point."

Billy took a towel from his bag and started wiping his thin face. "What kind of advertising do you work in, if you don't mind me asking?"

Briggs cleared his throat. "All kinds. Food and drink products mainly. One of my biggest projects was the Figroll biscuit ad on TV. You known the one that asks, 'How do you get the figs in the figroll?' "

The five of us started laughing and Briggs laughed along with us. "I know, I know, it's ridiculous, but it's one of the most successful ads on Irish television. It was my basic idea, but I wasn't given full credit for it. That's one of the reasons I'm quitting the business and going into another field. The music industry holds enormous potential, and I'm sure my experience in advertising will benefit me. More and more record companies and bands are realising the enormous power that advertising has. It can literally make or break a product."

I raised my head. "Music isn't just a product like food and drink!"

Briggs looked at me. "Of course it isn't. That's why I'm so excited about working with a band like yours. I love music, especially the soulful stuff that you play. It really gets me."

Hearn took a deep pull from his cigarette. "What kind of a cut would you be looking for, if we took you on?"

Briggs smiled. "You needn't worry on that score. I'd be willing to forego all commission for the first few months until I can demonstrate to you that I can substantially improve your earning capacity. After that, I'd expect the standard twenty per cent. But remember, if you're not happy with my performance in the first few months, you can drop me at any time and return the engagement ring, so to speak. But listen, it's very congested here. Why don't we go to a restaurant when you have your gear packed away, and we can discuss this in more detail over a steak before you hit the road back down the country. The meal's on me, by the way."

We finished changing our clothes and took down our musical equipment. When we went to load the van outside the club, we discovered that our four tyres had been slashed. Billy looked at me and cursed. "It must have been those bastards you had the run-in with earlier."

We gathered around the front of the van, cursing our luck. Hearn kicked one of the punctured tyres and spat on the road. "There goes the profit on tonight's gig. And we haven't a hope of getting a garage open on a Sunday night. What the hell are we going to do?"

Briggs stepped forward with his hands in his pockets. "You can stay in my pad in Leeson Street, if you like. I have only one bedroom, but you're welcome to sleep on the couch and armchairs in the living room. In the morning, I'll get you sorted out with some remoulds at a good price in a garage I know near my place."

A worried look came over Billy's face. "This means I'm going to miss school again tomorrow. My father'll eat me alive."

I looked at Billy. "I'm in the same boat. I've already had two warnings at the foundry because of the number of days I've missed, but to hell with them. I don't care if they sack me."

Hearn buttoned up his jacket. "The way I see it, we have to stay whether we like it or not. Now let's start putting the gear back into the club. It'll be safer there. Then we can go and eat."

While we were shifting the musical equipment back into the club Alfredo turned to Briggs and laughed. "By the way, I often wondered myself, how do they get the figs in the fig roll?"

"BAND LARK"

I've been all at sea in mutiny with my father
ON THE WATER

MY FATHER CLENCHED his fist and pounded the kitchen table, almost knocking his half-eaten bowl of tripe on the floor.

"I don't believe it! After all the trouble I went to to get you that job, and now you're going to turn your back on it, just like that! That band lark won't last a year, mark my words! What are you going to do then?"

I stepped back from the table, frightened by my father's anger. Not since he had taken his leather belt to me when I was eight or nine for stealing sweets from Toomey's grocery shop had I seen him so angry. He was purple in the face.

"I think you're wrong, Dad. We're very serious about the band. We practice three and four nights a week and we're beginning to get bookings all around the country. And now there's this German residency that we've been offered. We can't let the opportunity slip by."

My father smirked. "German residency! How much money are ye being paid for it?"

I hesitated. "Not a lot for this first trip, but if we do well we'll be booked back at twice the fee the next time. That's the way it works."

My father gave a false laugh. "That's a big *if*!"

"I really think we have a good chance of being successful, Dad. And lots of other people think so, too."

My father sneered. "Yeah, and I have a good chance of winning the pools or a treble at Fairyhouse. Grow up, son, will you!"

"Singing is what I want to do, Dad. I've given this a lot of thought, and I really think I can make a go of it."

"If you love it so much, why not just do it part-time like you've been doing up till now?"

"We'd always be second-best that way. You need to give it your full attention if you want to become successful in the music business."

My father looked across the room at my mother. "Have you nothing to say about this?"

My mother squeezed her hands. "There's no talking to him."

My father shoved his fingers through his hair. "You knew he was planning this, didn't you? He tells you everything."

My mother took a deep breath. "The first I learned of it was when he got in from work earlier this evening. I've been trying to talk him out of it since, but he won't listen to me. His says his mind's made up. He hates the foundry. He says he's not suited to it. But he's been saying that since he started there. You knew that yourself."

My father sneered. "Doesn't like it! That's a good one – he doesn't like working. Will you tell me who does? I certainly don't, but I have to do it. What else is going to put food on the table. Everyone has to work. And that job of his is a good solid job, unlike the back-breaking dead-end work I've had to do all my life. He could go anywhere in the world with a trade like that. Jesus, if you hadn't mollycoddled him all his life, he might have had a bit more grit in him."

My mother's face stiffened. She didn't say anything, but I could tell by her eyes that she deeply resented my father for having made this remark, and not just for herself but for me also.

I stared at my father. "There's no point in trying to throw the blame for this over on Mam. This is my decision and mine alone. And whether you like it or not, I'm going ahead with it. Even if the band doesn't work out, I still wouldn't want to be a turner. I have no interest in that kind of work. When you got me the job, I told you I didn't think I'd be suited to it, but you wouldn't listen to me. I'm not going back on this decision. I've handed in my notice, and that's that!"

My father pushed back his bowl of tripe – spilling half of it on the table-cloth – and got to his feet. "I've had enough of this! I'm getting out of here before I really lose my temper." He grabbed his jacket from the back of his chair and started to leave the room. When he reached the door, he turned round and glared at me. "Stay well clear of me from now on, mister! I don't want to see or hear you for many's the day. I've done all I can for you, and you've thrown it all back in my face. The sooner you move off out of here the better it will be for all of us. And when you land yourself in trouble in the future, don't come crying back to me. I'm finished with you!"

The front door slammed shut.

My mother sat at the head of the table. "He didn't mean half of what he said. Don't mind him. He's just worried about your future, and I am, too. This is a very big decision you're taking. You're still only sixteen, remember."

I could tell by the tone of her voice that she was on the verge of tears. It became too painful for me to remain in the room with her. A band meeting was planned for later that evening at Orlando's, so I used this as an excuse to make a quick exit from the house.

On my way downtown, I went into the Jesuits' chapel. There was a choir practising in the gallery. I knelt at the back of the church and started an Our Father. The hymn coming from above my head reminded me of a benediction service I'd attended years before when my father was away at sea. After the blessing, when the priest lowered the monstrance, the choir broke into 'Hail Queen of Heaven' and the opening lines made me think of my father and brought tears to my eyes: *Hail Queen of Heaven, the ocean star, guide of the wanderer here below. Thrown on life's surge, we claim thy care. Save us from peril and from woe.* Though the choir in the gallery above me now was singing a different hymn, the mournful tone of the melody almost had me in tears again.

After I left the church, I walked to the river. I sat on a bollard on the quayside just down from the harbour master's gate and looked out over the black night-water. It was cloudy, so there was very little visible, just the shadowy outline of a row of trees on the far bank. I started thinking of my father. I remembered a walk we'd made to the river together years before while he was home on leave from the sea. He was preoccupied with his own thoughts during most of the stroll, but when we reached the quayside he started asking me questions: "Do you know what a stevedore does, son?" "Yes, Dad. He takes the cargo from a ship." "Good boy. Now can you tell me what part of a ship is the starboard?" "Is it the right-hand side, Dad?" "It is, son. Very good. And the left is called the larboard or portside. I'll make a sailor of you yet."

The harbour clock rang out behind me. I looked back and saw that it was eight o'clock. I got to my feet and hurried off towards the city centre.

When I arrived at Orlando's, I found the four boys sitting at our usual table near the jukebox, drinking coffee and talking shop. Hearn was the first to spot me. "Where were you? I called to your house, but you were gone."

"I went for a walk."

Alfredo's eyes widened. "A what?!"

"A walk. You know, the thing you do with your feet."

Hearn stared at me. "What's up with you?"

I drew a deep breath. "I told my father about jacking in my job, and he blew a fuse. I had the worst row ever with him."

Billy cleared his throat. "I'm in the same boat. My old fella had a job all lined up for me in the ESB, if I got the Leaving. But we'll be in Germany now when the exams come up. The only way I managed to get him to agree to let me turn pro was to promise to go back to school next year or the year after if the band doesn't work out. But my mother's still not talking to me."

Hearn lit a cigarette and blew a smoke ring above Billy's head. "Listen, if ye keep this up ye'll have me in tears. My brother was going to get me a job up in the sausage factory, too, but you don't hear me moaning about it. Cheer up, for Christ's sake. The German tour starts in another few weeks. We'll be out of this town then and we won't be coming back. Now, let's get down to business!"

Mac sat forward. "Before you came, Johnny, we were discussing the idea of taking on that keyboard player who sat in with us last week at the gig in Dublin. It would be great to have the extra instrument for the German tour. It would make a huge difference to our sound."

Billy looked at me. "Alf and Hearn think he was a bit stiff. What do you think?"

I laughed. "He looked a bit like an altar boy all right, but he was terrific on the organ. And he's from down the country like us. I think we should get him. Let's take a vote on it."

FLOORED

In a grubby old bed, hungry for bread
And weighed down with care
ON THE WATER

WOKE AT dawn on the hard wooden floor of Briggs' living room beside the others with a cramp in my right arm. Though I was fully dressed, I was shivering from the cold because I was on the outside of the makeshift bed and someone had pulled the blankets from me during the night. Beside me, Peters, the band's new keyboard player, was wheezing in his sleep, and, inside him, Alfredo was scratching furiously under the covers. The others were sleeping peacefully.

I turned on my back and winced at the smell of shit coming from the bathroom adjoining the room we were lying in. The toilet in there was blocked, and there was shit in the bathtub as well. It had been like that since we'd moved in with Briggs almost three weeks before, after the German tour had fallen through.

I pulled a blanket over me and tried to return to sleep, but I couldn't manage it. As well as the cold and the smell, hunger pangs kept me awake. It had been a couple of days now since we'd eaten anything solid. Our last full meal, fish and chips, had been bought for us by Briggs' girl-friend Jacinta, a prostitute who lived on and off in the flat with Briggs.

The weak light coming through the curtainless window began to grow brighter. My eyes drifted around the room. Unlike the first time we'd stayed in the flat a few months earlier, the place hadn't a stick of furniture now. The sofa and armchairs that some of us had slept on back then were gone, as was the carpet from the floor and the pictures that had decorated the walls. Officially, Briggs wasn't supposed to be living in the flat any more. He hadn't paid rent for the place in over three months, and there were a number of notices to quit lying on top of the mantelpiece beside another bundle of pawnbrokers' tickets for the furniture.

Peters woke on the floor beside me and took a pair of spectacles from the inside pocket of his jacket, which he'd been using as a pillow. After he settled the glasses on his nose, he squinted and yawned. "How about getting some milk before it gets too bright, Johnny?"

"OK."

The two of us got out from under the blankets and tiptoed downstairs. Outside in Leeson Street there wasn't a soul about. Peters pointed to some milk bottles standing by a red door across the street. "Let's get them from that side of the road today. It's not fair to be always taking them from this side."

"You're an honest thief, Peters."

We took two bottles from the red doorway and moved on to other buildings where we collected four more pints between us. With our arms full, we hurried back to our own building, hoping we hadn't been seen by anyone in the neighbourhood.

On the way upstairs Peters started laughing. "It's hard to believe that just a few short weeks ago I had a good steady job in the GPO and lived in a nice comfortable flat. And now here I am squatting and turning into a common thief. I swear, before this I never stole a thing in my life."

I looked at Peters. He was at least five years older than me but didn't look it.

"I did a fair bit of stealing myself in my younger years, more for the thrill than anything else."

Peters smiled. "It's exciting all right, but I wish it wasn't so necessary. I was thinking of writing home to my sister in New Ross and asking her to send me some money, but I'd be afraid she'd tell my mother and father."

"You haven't been home since you quit your job?"

"I couldn't face telling my father that I was joining a band, so I wrote home instead. I had a letter from my mother just before I left my flat a month ago. She took the news calmly enough, but she told me my father was hopping mad. If he could see the way we're living here now, he'd really flip."

"My old man's the same. He didn't even say goodbye to me when I was leaving home. That was only three weeks ago, imagine. It feels like an eternity the way we've been living here, doesn't it?"

Peters squinted over the rims of his glasses. "Yeah, but things are bound to improve in a few weeks when we start gigging again."

"I hope so. I felt like crying last night I was so hungry."

"Me, too."

Back in the room, the clinking sound of the bottles woke the others. The four of them sat up with the blankets tucked up around their chins, staring hungrily at the milk in our hands. We gave them a bottle each and kept a bottle each for ourselves, then got back under the covers.

While we were drinking the milk, Alfredo turned to me. "You didn't hear a loud roar last night, did you? It really frightened the hell out of me."

I shook my head. "Maybe it was Briggs having a row with Jacinta?"

Alfredo shook his head. "She usually doesn't get in till around three in the morning. This was just after one. I remember looking at my watch. Anyway, it was a man's voice I heard."

Hearn gulped back some milk and belched. "It was probably Briggs and his cronies having another one of them seances. The sooner we get the fuck out of this kip the better. How did we ever get involved with that wanker anyway, will you tell me that?"

Peters turned to Hearn. "To be fair to him, it wasn't his fault that the club in Frankfurt went bankrupt."

Hearn belched. "No, but he might have checked things out a bit more with the agent before he made the booking, the bollix!"

Billy drew a loud breath. "There's no point in going over all that again. We know he cocked up. Let's leave it at that. We'll be dumping him as soon as we're in a position to get out of this shit hole."

We sat drinking the milk in silence for a few moments; then Alfredo groaned. "I'd give anything for a smoke. The minute I started drinking the milk, I got the longing. I always love a ciggy after a meal."

Hearn cursed. "What's the point in saying that? You did the same thing yesterday morning. We'd all love a fag, but whining isn't going get it for us."

Alfredo scratched his knuckles. "Who's whining? I was just saying it would be nice, that's all." Billy drank back the last of his milk and got out from under the blankets. After placing his empty bottle in a corner at the other side of the room, he came back and started taking down his trousers. Hearn looked up at him and cursed. "Not while we're drinking our milk, Billy!"

Billy went on lowering his jeans. A huge boil became visible on his left leg, right in the centre of the calf muscle. He looked down at it for a moment and smiled. "I think it's beginning to burst. There's some pus oozing from the head. That's a sure sign that it's on the mend. It's still very sore, though."

Alfredo cursed. "Put it away, for Christ sake! We don't want to see it any more. We're sick of it!"

Mac cleared his throat. "Yeah, Billy, not today. My stomach's in knots as it is. Pull up your jeans and come back to bed."

Billy started pulling up his trousers, slowly so as not to rub the material against the swelling. When he got back under the blankets, he turned to Alfredo and cursed. "If you start scratching yourself again, you dirty little wop, I'll kick you out on the floor! You must be infested. You kept me awake half the night tearing at your balls."

"I can't help it. I'm itchy as hell."

Hearn moved away from Alfredo. "I hope it's not the scabies you've got. They're highly contagious. I got them once in school, and it's a bugger trying to get rid of them."

We finished the milk, stretched out on the floor and tried to go back to sleep. After a lot of tossing and turning, the five boys managed to nod off, but I found it impossible to sleep myself. I lay awake for over an hour until it was fully bright; then I got up and went to the kitchen.

There was no food in the cupboards, just a packet of tea bags that we'd bought the week before when we still had a little money. I boiled the kettle and made a cup of tea, using the dregs of the stolen milk to whiten it.

While I was sipping the tea at the kitchen table, the door opened and Briggs' girlfriend Jacinta came into the room dressed in Briggs' paisley dressing gown. When she saw me, she put her hand to her neck to cover her exposed cleavage. "Janey, you're up early. Do you mind if I join you for a quick cuppa. I'm parched. I have to go out to me ma's in Finglas this mornin'. Me brother Ger's makin' his first holy communion. If I don't show my face, I'll be kilt."

Jacinta made herself a cup of tea and sat opposite me. She took a packet of Rothmans from the pocket of the dressing gown and offered me one. It had been a couple of days since I'd last smoked, so the cigarette tasted sour and made me slightly dizzy.

We sat in silence drinking the tea for a few moments. Jacinta looked at me over the rim of her cup. "I hope you don't mind me sticking my nose into your business, but why don't you and your band go home? Yous're fading away to nothing here."

I put down my cup. "We couldn't do that. We gave up jobs and school to go to Germany, most of us against our parents' wishes. Billy even ran away from home. We couldn't face them after what's happened."

Jacinta took a pull from her cigarette. "I'm sure your mas and das would love to see you, no matter what."

I laughed. "I don't think so, not my old man anyway. But we'll be all right. We have some gigs coming up in a week or so. We'll have some money then. The only reason we went this low is because we had no bookings lined up for the month we were supposed to be in Germany. Once the gigs pick up, we'll be in a position to start renting our own flat. Then we'll be fine."

"I still think yous're wrong to stay here. It's not healthy with the toilet the way it is. I don't know how many times I said it to Mikey, but he doesn't seem to know what he's doing lately. He's very confused."

Jacinta finished her tea and went back to Briggs' bedroom. She returned to the kitchen a few minutes later dressed in a gaudy blue dress with her hair backcombed and her eyes darkened with eye shadow. She had left her cigarettes on the table, so I thought she'd come back for them, but when I tried to hand her the pack she told me to keep them. Then she took three pound notes from her purse and placed them on the table in front of me. "That should get you and the boys something proper to eat. Don't tell Mikey I gave it to yous. I have to dash now or I'll miss me brother's big day. See you later."

"Thanks, Jacinta. You're very generous."

"You can pay me back when you're famous."

Soon after Jacinta left, I went off and bought some groceries in a nearby shop. When I returned to the flat, I started cooking breakfast.

The smell of sizzling rashers and sausages drew the boys to the kitchen.

Hearn was the first to arrive. "Where the hell did the grub come from? It smells divine. And what's this on the table. Twenty Rothmans! Did you rob a bank or what?"

"Jacinta gave them to me, as well as the money to buy the food."

Hearn grinned. "She must have done well on the game last night."

I gave Hearn a stern look and turned back to the frying pan.

While the six of us were sitting around the table eating the fry, Billy turned at me with his mouth full of sausage. "When I saw that my boil was on the mend this morning, I knew our luck was going to turn. Pass me the bread there, Johnny. And if you're not eating those rasher rinds, I'll have them."

A peal of bells from a nearby church started ringing. Peters raised his head from his plate and readjusted the glasses on his nose. "I'd forgotten, it's Sunday. Who's coming to mass?"

Hearn stuffed some rasher into his mouth. "Not me. I'm going back to bed after this."

Mac, Billy and Alfredo kept eating without saying a word.

The bells went on ringing. I looked down at the bread in my hand, then turned to Peters. "I'll go with you."

THE SACRIFICE

Shot down just when I thought I was flying
Hit the ground so hard I thought I was dying
SHOT DOWN

HE PET-SHOP OWNER looked at Billy and me across the counter. "No, we don't sell white doves, or any other doves for that matter. Would a budgie not do you?"

Billy looked at me. I shook my head. "No, it's a white dove we want."

The pet-shop owner rubbed his chin. "I could give you the address of a pigeon keeper in Finglas who might be able to help you. I'm not sure if he keeps white doves, but he sold a pigeon once to one of my regular customers. I think I still have his address in my notebook. Wait here a minute and I'll get it for you."

The man went into a back office and returned a few moments later with a piece of paper in his hand. "Here. I've written it out for you. The pigeon keeper's name is Frank, and he lives at this address. He might be able to help you. Tell him I sent you."

We left the shop and got back into our van.

Behind the wheel, Hearn blew a fuse when I handed him the address and told him to drive to Finglas. "All that way, for a bloody dove? You must be mad!"

Peters squinted. "It's a bit far, Johnny. Are you sure this idea of your is going to be worth it? Tell us about it again."

I shook my head. "I told you twice already. Before the end of the gig tonight, when we have the crowd with us, we'll release the dove on stage as a symbol of freedom. I'm telling you, they'll go mad for it."

Peters looked at me. "But where will the dove fly to? The Scene Club is in a basement with a low ceiling."

I rubbed my neck. "It's bound to find somewhere to perch, and we'll release it when the gig's over."

Alfredo laughed. "It's such a daft idea, I think it might work."

Billy widened his eyes. "I think it's a brainwave. It's just the kind of gimmick we need to make a name for ourselves."

I looked at Billy. "I didn't think of it as a gimmick!"

Hearn cursed and switched on the engine. "Whatever the hell it is, it better be worth all this trouble you're putting us to. Two pet shops already and now all the way out to Finglas! We'll be late for the gig at this rate."

When we arrived at the address in Finglas, Billy accompanied me to the front door. A woman with rollers in her hair answered the bell. I asked to see Frank. A few minutes later, a man in a soiled vest came out chewing a match. I mentioned the pet-shop owner, then asked Frank if he had a white dove he might sell us as a pet. Frank scratched his chest. "I don't have a pure white bird, but I have one almost white. Come on into the back and have a look."

Frank's small backyard was taken up almost entirely by handmade wooden pigeon coops, most of them raised off the ground sitting on concrete blocks. The birds in them started cooing loudly when they heard us coming. Frank laughed. "They think they're going to be fed again, the fools." He opened one of the wire-mesh doors and took out a light-grey coloured pigeon. "That's as near to white as I have. Any good to you?"

Billy turned to me. "It's almost white."

In the evening light the bird didn't look a bit white to me, but I decided it was better than nothing. "How much?"

Frank rubbed his chest. "As it isn't exactly what you're looking for, it's yours for ten bob."

We left the house with the pigeon in a cardboard box and got into the van. While we were driving back to town, Alfredo and Peters asked to see the bird. I opened one of the cardboard flaps and put my hand inside the box. Alfredo gave a nervous titter. "Are you not afraid it might peck the fingers off you?"

I could feel the pigeon's wings trying to expand as I put my hand around its warm body. "I used to have a pigeon myself once. I found it in the street with a broken wing. I took it home and kept it in our shed. My father put a splint on the injured wing, and when it healed I released it. They're harmless creatures."

I took the pigeon out of the box and held it up with my two hands. Its neck was bobbing backwards and forwards, and its tiny eyes kept jerking in its head. Hearn glanced back at the bird and pulled a long face. "That's not a white dove!"

Billy leaned forward. "It'll do. It was the whitest he had."

Back in town, we bought a roll of tinfoil in a grocery shop and covered the box with it to make it look decorative. We arrived at the Scene Club just after eight and spent an hour setting up our musical equipment and running over songs. Just before the club opened, we put the silver box on a small table beside Mac's vox amplifier and readjusted one of the stage lights to shine down on it.

Soon after nine-thirty, we went on stage. Already there was quite a large crowd in the club, many of them staring up at the silver box. While the band were checking their tuning, I stepped up to the microphone. "If you're wondering what's in the box, you'll have to wait till later to find out. Meanwhile, we're kicking off with 'Ain't Too Proud to Beg'."

We played five or six up-tempo numbers and then slowed things down with one of our show-stoppers, 'When a Man Loves a Woman'. When the audience recognised the organ intro, they stopped dancing and looked up at the stage. Though I had enjoyed singing this song when we first included it in our set some months before, I was beginning to find it a bit melodramatic by this stage. Still, when the band brought it to a crashing close, the applause was loud and long. We played another three or four fast songs and took a break.

In the dressing room, Peters tackled Alfredo for losing the beat in a few of the numbers. Alfredo puffed on a cigarette and took the criticism without defending himself.

Back on stage, we accelerated the pace and played flat out for more than an hour. By the end of the night, most of the fellas in the crowd were jumping about with their shirts open and their chests exposed. After announcing our final song, 'Iko Iko', I told the audience to keep their eyes on the silver box.

Halfway through the number, I noticed that steam was beginning to rise off the dancers at the front of the stage. A sea of hands was waving in the air and dozens of bulging eyes were staring up at me. I started chanting scat words into the microphone, and the audience repeated them:

"Inaw."

"INAW."

"Chawah."

"CHAWAH."

"Ooooo."

"OOOOOO."

I gestured to the band to take the volume down. Mac stopped playing his guitar. Peters held a low, dissonant chord on his organ, while Billy played a single pulse note on his bass. The crowd started swaying back-wards and forwards to the descending beat of Alfredo's tom-toms. I put my mouth to microphone and started breathing heavily.

"Are you ready?"

"YEAH!"

"Let me hear it louder!"

"YEAHHHHHHHH!"

I looked back at the band. Peters ran his fingers rapidly up and down his keys, creating a deafening crescendo of noise. Mac slashed at his Tele-caster and turned the body of the guitar on his amplifier. A roar of feed-back wailed up from the speakers. Alfredo started pounding on his tom-toms, and Billy began to slap the low strings of his bass guitar with his open hand. The crowd started leaping in the air and throwing their arms about.

I raised my hand and brought the volume of the music down again. The crowd calmed down. I put my mouth back to the microphone and groaned. "Do you want to see what's in the box?"

"YEAHH!"

"Do you really want to see what's in the box?"

"YEAHHHHHHHHH!"

I stepped back to the table and teased the audience by doing snake movements with my arm above the silver box. A few dancers strained forward to get a better look. I pressed my hand through the cardboard flaps. The band stopped playing. I gripped the bird between my fingers and raised it slowly out of the box. A gasp of surprise went up at the front of the stage when the bird became visible. People further back crushed forward. The club went suddenly quiet. I put my free hand around the bird's breast and raised it above my head. Then I stepped back to the microphone and roared. "FREEDOM!"

Alfredo's cymbals crashed behind me. I released my grip on the bird. Its wings fluttered above my head, and it flew out of my open hands and down over the heads of the audience. A huge roar went up in the club, and the crowd turned and watched the free flight of the bird. It disappeared into the darkness at the opposite end of the club. For a few moments, no one moved; then someone in the middle of the crowd gave a loud yell and started running after the bird. The rest of the audience followed suit.

From the stage, I couldn't see very clearly what was going on at the back of the club, but the noise of the crowd began to alarm me. I tried to calm things down, but my pleas were ignored. For a few minutes, there was pandemonium as people ran backwards and forwards after the bird. Then an eerie silence descended on the club and a single scream went up. Moments later the crowd started shuffling back to the front of the stage. As they came towards me, I noticed that one of the fellas at the front of the crowd had the bird in his hands. When he got closer, I saw that his bare chest was covered in blood; then I noticed that the pigeon between his fingers was headless. I shuddered behind the microphone. The fella holding the decapitated bird came forward and held it towards me. Without realising what I was doing, I took it from him. Looking down at the bleeding entrails around the bloody neck, I felt sick in the stomach. I looked out at the crowd. They stared back at me, waiting for me to do something. For a moment, I thought of leaving the stage, but I knew if I did this the night would be a complete failure. I took a deep breath and held the dead bird up in the air. A huge roar went up in the club, and the band behind me started playing. The yelling of the crowd and the loud music went to my head. I started dancing and waving the headless pigeon in the air. The audience went wild. For a few crazy minutes, I hopped around the stage like a demented witchdoctor; then I ran out of breath and began to feel dizzy. The dead bird dropped out of my hand. My legs grew weak. I stopped dancing and collapsed.

When I regained consciousness, I was on the floor at the front of the stage with a large group of people standing around me. Billy, Peters and Hearn were asking the crowd to stand back. Billy and Peters picked me up and started leading me out of the club. While they were helping me through the audience, a dark-haired girl came towards me. "Are you all right, Johnny? Are you all right?" I recognised her face but couldn't remember her name. In a lane beside the club the week before she had masturbated me beside some dustbins. Her face drifted away in the crowd.

Outside the club, Billy and Peters helped me into the back of our van. Hearn got in behind the wheel and switched on the engine. "We'd better take you to a hospital for a check-up."

Peters got into the back seat beside Billy. "Baggot Street is the nearest. I'll give you directions."

While we were driving through town, Hearn looked back at me and shook his head. "You and your bloody white dove!"

Peters laughed. "It certainly caused a stir, that's for sure."

Billy nodded. "I'll bet our name will get around after this."

While the boys were helping me into Casualty, I looked down at my hands and noticed that they were covered in blood.

MARY

I knew that she really loved me
I knew by the way she kissed me
But I didn't really love her, I realised
MARY

ARY WAS WAITING for me by the bandstand on Dún Laoghaire pier, a regular meeting place of ours since we'd started going out together soon after the band moved to the area. Back then I had been infatuated with her innocent good looks, but now as I approached her and automatically took the hand she offered me, my only concern was how I was going to break it off with her without hurting her feelings. Already I had chickened out of doing this two nights in a row. I was determined to go ahead with it tonight.

"Sorry I'm late. The band got into a long discussion after rehearsals about a fella we're considering taking on as our manager. He's calling to the flat later tonight for a meeting."

Mary squeezed my hand. "That's OK. I only got here myself a few minutes ago." This was a lie, but a lie told for the best of intentions, to let me off the hook. I found this generosity of Mary's annoying. I would have preferred if she showed a little anger from time to time, but she never did.

We started walking out the pier hand in hand. The sky above us had clear blue patches, but it was a very windy evening. Many of the other strollers on the pier were holding on to hats, coats and dresses to protect them from the strong breeze. Mary had no such problem with her clothes; she was dressed in black cord jeans with a buttoned-up black cardigan on top. She often dressed in dark tones like this, a little like a novice nun. When we met first, I had been attracted by this severe lack of colour (even her face was pale), but later I began to hope that she might show up in something a little brighter from time to time. Now I didn't much care one way or the other.

I looked across the harbour to where the mailboat was preparing to embark on its night sailing to Holyhead. The reason I liked coming to the pier at this time was to watch the ferry undocking (old habits run deep). As I looked at the ship, the lower half of which was obscured by some customs' buildings, its siren let out a shrill blast to indicate that it would soon be departing. A flock of gulls rose up from the roof of the customs' sheds and hovered in the sky above the ship.

I turned back to Mary. "It's a three-year contract we'll have to sign. That's why we're having discussions. We don't want to end up with someone like our last manager. This fellow – Trench is his name – seems a lot more efficient. He was in a band himself at one time, so he knows the score."

Mary glanced at me. "How did you meet him?"

"In a club he manages in town. We played there a few weeks back, but it was only the other night that he put the proposition to us. He says he has some good contacts abroad. His aim is to move us to London, where he reckons we could do really well."

Mary looked across the harbour towards the mailboat, which had just given a second blast of its siren. "It won't be long so till you'll be taking that route across the Irish sea yourselves."

I thought for a moment and took a deep breath. "We've always known that we'd have to leave Ireland eventually if we want to find real success. I told you that when I met you. But I'm sure you'll find someone else when I'm gone."

Mary's grip on my hand tightened. She didn't say anything, but I could tell that she was on the verge of tears. I focused on the mailboat, which was just beginning to pull away from its moorings.

By the time we reached the end of the pier, the mailboat was out at sea. I left Mary standing on the lower section of the walkway and climbed up on to the granite parapet just back from the beacon tower. While I was watching the departing ship and taking the full brunt of the breeze, I glanced back towards the coastline. I could just about make out the line of old terraced houses on the seafront where the band were now living. Our flat was above a tearoom that operated during the summer season, which hadn't yet arrived. Since moving there, the band's luck had changed dramatically. We were now playing three and sometimes four nights a week, and we had a growing following around the Dublin club circuit.

When I got down from the parapet, Mary offered me her hand and we headed back to Dún Laoghaire. We spent an hour in a coffee shop on the main street listening to the jukebox and sipping coffee, then we headed home.

On the way to Mary's place, we came to a leafy avenue of tall detached houses with large gardens before them. After our first date, Mary had told me that she lived in one of these big houses. We had spent the best part of an hour talking and kissing outside its large iron gate. A few nights later, on our second date, Mary broke down and told me that she didn't live in the big house at all but in a much smaller semi-detached close by.

After we bypassed Mary's fantasy home, we came to a narrow laneway that led to the estate where she really lived. We stopped at our usual parting place, and Mary waited for me to start kissing her. For a moment I felt tempted to put my arms around her and manoeuvre her back against the brick wall for one last fling of innocent pleasure, but I stopped myself.

"I'd better go."

Mary lowered her chin. "I don't have to be in for a another few minutes."

"I need to get back to the flat for the meeting I was telling you about."

"When will I see you again?"

I hesitated. "I'm not sure. We're playing tomorrow night. I don't know how we're fixed after that. I have to go now, though, really. Goodnight."

When I got to the end of the lane I looked back. Mary was still standing at the spot where I'd left her, staring after me. I waved and walked off, relieved that I'd managed to get away without committing myself to another date.

93

When I arrived at the flat, the downstairs part of the building (the tea room) was in total darkness, but there was light showing through a chink in the curtains of one of the upstairs windows. As I let myself in the front door, a heavy wave crashed on the rocky shoreline behind me.

Upstairs I found Hearn, Mac and Peters sitting around a glowing fire in the living room, deep in conversation.

"Ye look very serious there, lads. What are ye talking about?"

Hearn glanced back at me from the couch. "We were discussing you, actually. Mac was just saying how much of a bollix you are."

Mac laughed. "Don't mind him, Johnny. We were talking about Alf's drumming."

Hearn shifted his position on the couch to let me sit down. "Peters was just making the point that his timing is still all over the place. No matter how many times we speak to him about it, he just doesn't seem able to improve. If Trench takes us on and we move to London, we don't think he's going to be able to cut the mustard."

After my evening of scheming to get out of one relationship, I didn't feel up to the type of conspiracy that was hatching here. I looked at Mac. "Where's Alf now?"

"At the pictures uptown with Billy. They should be home soon."

Hearn lit a cigarette. "We know it's going to be tough on him, but the three of us agree we're going to have to find a replacement soon. What do you think?"

I hesitated. "I agree, but I don't think we should be talking about it now. Trench will be here soon. We should be concentrating on him, shouldn't we?"

Peters looked at me over the rims of his glasses. "You're right, but we're going to have to face the problem sooner or later. We can't go on the way things are. It just won't do."

I hopped up from the couch and threw some coal on the fire. While I was washing my hands in the kitchen, Billy and Alfredo arrived home. Alfredo was in good spirits. He made a pot of tea and produced a packet of biscuits that he'd bought on the way back to the flat. "Here, take two, Johnny. They're the chocolate ones you like."

While we were munching the biscuits and drinking the tea, there was a sudden screech of brakes outside the house. Hearn went to the window.

"It's Trench. He's a real show-off in that sports car, isn't he? Now remember, don't act overenthusiastic. We don't want to give him the impression that we're a pushover."

Hearn went downstairs to open the front door and returned a few moments later with Trench, a good-looking fella in his mid-twenties in a grey mohair suit. He came into the room with a cigarette dangling from his mouth, smiling at something Hearn had said to him on the way upstairs. Hearn was also grinning.

"I was just saying to Stirling Moss here: with a car like that, it's a wonder he hasn't got a good-looking bird hanging out of his sleeve all the time."

Trench laughed. "I usually do, but I wouldn't bring her to this den of iniquity. I hope you haven't been overdoing it with the gargle again, lads?"

During our meeting with Trench a few nights earlier, a lot of drink had been consumed. Alfredo, Billy and myself ended up getting drunk and going for a midnight swim in the sea across from the flat with our clothes on.

Alfredo held up his cup. "It's just tea tonight. Would you like a cup?"

"No, thanks." Trench stood in front of the fireplace. "I'm sorry to have kept you so late, but I couldn't get away from the club till now. I'll be glad to pack that place in. The bread's good, but the hours are the pits. But enough about my problems. I hope you've given some consideration to what we were discussing the last time I was here. To recap: my main point was that I'd only be interested in taking you on if you're willing to make the move across the water. This country's a dead loss; there's just not enough punters here. If you're interested in the big reddies, then we have to set our sights across the pond. I have a few contacts in Scotland and England who'll help us get a foot in the door. But remember, it won't be easy making an impression over there. We'll be starting at the bottom."

CAGED

In the spotlight above my chords
Singing for rewards, it's a lonely life
With my stomach full of butterflies
Waiting for applause to rise, I'm on the edge of a knife
THE SPIDER

WHEN WE ENTERED the hall at the back of the Tartan Arms, Jay, the band's new drummer, was the first to notice that the stage was surrounded by thick iron bars. "Shit, look at this, lads, a cage! How are we supposed to get the gear in there?"

Hearn went up to the bars and gave them a rattle. "I hope we're not going to have a lion tamer as a support act tonight."

Trench threw a half-smoked cigarette on the floor and stood on it. "I don't like the look of this. I'd better go and get an explanation from the manager. Wait here while I go to the bar out front and try and find him."

Trench left the hall and returned a few minutes later with a small, fat, red-faced Scotsman. "Boys, this is Hamish, the manager of the place. He's going to open the cage so that you can get the gear on stage. The cage, by the way, is for your protection. Hamish has been telling me that the club gets a little rowdy on Saturday nights."

Hamish laughed. "Aye, it does that. But don't worry, boys, you'll be perfectly safe inside them bars. They're almost an inch thick. Once I lock you in there, no one will be able to touch you."

Hamish took a large key from his jacket pocket and inserted it in a lock in the middle of the cage. I cleared my throat. "You mean you're actually going to lock us in there while we're playing?"

Hamish pushed open a section of the cage. "It's for your own safety, laddie. In the three years I've been managing this place, we've never had a musician hurt. When you see how wild things get here tonight, you'll realise that that's quite an achievement. And it's all thanks to these safety bars."

Peters shook his head. "But isn't it dangerous locking us in? What if a fire broke out or something?"

"Och, don't be frettin' yourself. There's a wee exit door at the back of the stage. You'll be able to get out through that in an emergency. And there'll be an ambulance on duty outside the club from ten o'clock."

Trench's eyes widened. "An ambulance?!"

"Aye. They used to wait until we called them out, but it became such a regular occurrence they started coming of their own accord, to be prepared. They have all the medical stuff they need in the van for most patch-up jobs. They only take the people with serious injuries like broken limbs to hospital. Occasionally they have to call in a back-up team from Drumcacklin, a few miles over the hills, but that's usually only necessary on special occasions like New Year's Eve or Easter Sunday or when the local football team win a championship, which isn't very often I can tell you."

We looked at one another and lowered our eyes. In the two weeks we'd been touring Scotland, we had played in some hairy places, but this took the biscuit.

We set up our musical equipment inside the cage and ran through a few songs; then we drove off to a local B&B that had been booked for us.

We arrived back at the Tartan Arms just before nine-thirty, our scheduled time for going on stage. We had already changed into our stage clothes, so we didn't bother going to the dressing room. Hamish escorted us straight through the hall – which was already beginning to fill up – and locked us inside the stage area with his key. "Give them lots of dance tunes and you'll have no problems."

While the band were checking their tuning and settling themselves on stage, I went to the lead microphone and looked out at the audience, most of whom were grouped round the bar at the back of the hall. I cleared my throat. "Good evening. It's nice to be here in the Grampian Highlands. This is our first time playing behind bars, but I swear we're innocent, your honour."

A few people laughed in the bar area. I breathed a sigh of relief and raised the microphone a little on its stand. "We hear you like dancing, so we're going to kick off with a few hornpipes." Two or three people glanced at me with blank expressions. I laughed into the mike. "Only joking. We'll start with a song by Curtis Mayfield called 'Move On Up'."

The moment the band began to play, the dance floor started filling up. At the end of our first number, we received a good round of applause. This put us somewhat at ease. We launched into 'Dancing in the Street' and more dancers filed on to the floor.

An hour sailed by without incident. I announced that we were taking a ten-minute break. Hamish came and let us out of the cage and walked us to the dressing room. "You're doing great, laddies. Keep it lively; that's what they go for up here."

Five minutes after we returned to the stage, a fight broke out in the bar area. The lights went up. From the elevated position of the stage, we had a clear view of the scrap. There were only three or four individuals involved but they made a hell of a racket, overturning tables and chairs while flailing their fists at one another. Within the space of a few minutes, it was over, broken up by a small team of hefty bouncers. The lights in the hall were turned down again. The couples on the dance floor resumed dancing, and the drinkers at the bar turned back to their glasses. I took a deep breath and went on singing.

Ten minutes later, another fight started right in front of the cage. A red-haired dancer was set upon by a fella who struck him on the jaw for no apparent reason. The victim retaliated. A few girls yelped and jumped back. The lights were turned up again. Bouncers came from every corner of the hall to try and break up the fight, but most of them ended up becoming involved in it themselves. Within minutes half the male dancers on the floor were at one another's throats while their female partners looked on wide-eyed from both sides of the hall. On stage we moved back from the bars and kept playing.

A few minute into the fight, a fella was knocked to the floor and didn't get up. One of the bouncers rushed to an emergency exit and pushed the bars open. Moments later a couple of stretcher-bearers in uniform rushed into the hall and whisked the unconscious victim away on a canvas stretcher. I looked across the stage at Peters and threw my eyes up to the ceiling. The band went on playing.

The stretcher-bearers were kept on their toes right up until we played our final song at eleven-thirty. Then Hamish came and let us out of the cage. "You did well under pressure, boys. It was a wee bit fierier than usual tonight, but there were no serious injuries. Get yourselves a drink at the bar before it closes. It's on the house. You'll be safe enough now. Most of the troublemakers are gone."

Peters and myself went to the bar and ordered a couple of pints of bitter. A girl with tight-cropped hair approached us and congratulated Peters on our performance. "They don't appreciate good music up here in the High-lands. All they're interested in is beer and fighting. My friend Gwen and I aren't from these parts. We're just camping here for the weekend, a mile out the road. That's Gwen smiling at me from the table across the way. You can join us, if you like. My name's Mags."

I could tell by the gleam in Peters' eye that he fancied Mags. I looked across at her friend. Gwen had long auburn hair and an attractive smile. We went across to the table. I sat beside Gwen. "Hi, I'm Johnny and he's John. Your friend Mags here was telling us you're camping outside the town?"

Gwen smiled and lowered her eyes. "Mmm."

Mags laughed. "Johnny and John! That must be confusing for you?"

Peters squinted. "They call me by my second name. Actually, there are three Johns in the band. Our guitarist is Johnny, too, but we call him Mac, which is part of his surname, McMahon."

Mags laughed. "I thought Ireland was a land of Micks and Paddies. I love your accent, by the way. What part of Ireland are you from?"

Peters shifted the glasses on his nose. "Most of the band are from Limerick, but I'm from a place called New Ross, and our drummer, Jay, is from Dublin. He only joined us a few weeks back, just before we came to Scotland. Before that we had an Italian drummer."

I glanced at Peters. "He wasn't Italian, actually. He was born in Limer-ick and he thought of himself as Irish."

Peters looked at me and turned away.

Mags ran her finger round the rim of her beer glass. "Where are you playing next?"

Peters sat forward. "Tonight's our last night in Scotland. We play New-castle, Manchester and Birmingham next week, then we're off to Germany for a fortnight's tour. After that we're going to base ourselves in Swinging London."

I offered Gwen a cigarette. "What part of Scotland are ye from?"

Gwen shook her head to indicate that she didn't smoke. Mags turned to me. "A place called Kirkcaldy, a godforsaken spot south of here on the east coast. I'd love to live in London myself. I often dream of moving there."

Peters swallowed some beer. "Why don't you then?"

"Och, I wouldn't have the nerve to just up and go on my own. I'm hoping Gwen will come with me someday, but she's a bit of a homebird. Aren't you, Gwen?"

"Mmm."

The shutters came down on the bar, and the bouncers started asking people to leave. I was becoming a little irritated by Gwen's silence, so I finished my drink and stood up. "I'll go and help the others take down the gear. Goodnight, girls."

Peters drank back the last of his beer and stood up. "I'd better go with you or they'll be calling me a shirker."

Mags got to her feet and smiled at Peters. "That's a pity. We were just beginning to enjoy your company. Now we're going to have to walk out a dark lonely road all by ourselves. We were frightened out of our wits going back to the tent last night. Weren't we, Gwen?"

Gwen nodded and rose from the table.

Peters looked at me and turned to Mags. "We'll walk you out, if you like? Won't we, Johnny?"

I hesitated. "Sure. Just give us a few minutes till we help the lads pack away the gear. A midnight stroll would be nice."

Outside the village it was pitch dark. We followed a narrow winding road between high hills for well over a mile, and still there was no sign of the girls' tent. It started to rain. I had a jacket, but Peters was wearing only a light pullover. Mags took off her anorak and invited him to take shelter under it. "It's not far now, just up here a few hundred yards."

We had to scale a wall and trudge through a muddy field to reach the spot where the girls were camped. The tent was small, but the four of us piled in to get out of the rain. After a long search in the dark, Mags located a torch but then discovered that the batteries were dead. "Och, I knew there was something I should have done today. We'll have to sit in the dark now. If this rain keeps up, you two are going to have to stay the night. You can share our sleeping bags, but no funny stuff."

The rain grew heavier. The girls got into their sleeping bags with most of their clothes on, and we joined them. Though Gwen was thin, it was a tight squeeze getting into the single sleeping bag with her. Once inside I became aroused. I put my arm around her and pressed my mouth to her lips. While we were kissing, I ran my hand over her small breasts and then lowered it to the front of her jeans. Gwen suddenly drew back and put her mouth to my ear. "I'm in my flowers, I'm afraid." I jerked back, surprised not by Gwen's words but by the deep bass tone of her voice. In the dark, it was almost as if I was lying with a man. I said a quick goodnight, resettled my head on the hard ground and tried to go to sleep. Eventually I managed to nod off.

Sometime in the middle of the night, Mags woke me. "You and Gwen are going to have to shift. The rain's coming in at our side of the tent."

Before I had a chance to move, Gwen's deep baritone rumbled like thunder beside me: "Ochhhhhhh, it's coming in here, too. We're all going to have to move to the back of the tent or we'll be saturated."

Over the next few hours, the four of us shifted backwards and forwards trying to avoid the incoming rain. In the end we gave up and lay back on the waterlogged sleepingbags and waited for dawn to arrive.

Soon after it started growing bright, the rain stopped. The four of us got out of the tent and started squeezing the water from our clothes. There were high craggy hills all around us dotted with sheep. I gazed up a long misty valley. A huge mountain range jutting into the sky took my breath away. "What a terrific place! It would almost make you want to go off and become a shepherd."

Peters squinted. "I can barely see through these blasted lenses; they're all fogged up from the damp."

Mags dragged the two wet sleeping bags out of the tent and threw them across a wide granite boulder. "We won't be able to sleep till these things dry out. We may as well walk back as far as the village with you. At least you'll be able to get a few hours sleep in your B&B before you move on."

As we approached the village, bells rang out from a small grey chapel on a hill. We made our way to the stone building and were surprised to discover that it was a Catholic church. Peters looked through one of the porch doors. "Mass seems to be starting."

I dipped my finger in a holy water font. "Will we go in?"

Mags laughed. "I never heard of rock musicians going to church."

Peters smiled. "Come on in with us."

Mags shook her head. "But we're Protestants."

Peters pushed open the door. "That doesn't matter."

The two girls looked at one another and smiled; then the four of us stepped into the quiet, half-empty church and walked up the echoing aisle.

THE REVELLES

And another night of telling tales
Of nights spent with ripe females
FOURTH SKIN BLUES

"*V*ER BEERS UNT *einen viskey und soda, bitte.*"

The hotel barman looked at me in bewilderment. "*Was ist dass?*"

After the six or seven beers I'd drunk since returning from the Razz Club, I was a little fuzzy headed. I took a deep breath and tried to recall other German words I'd picked up during our first day in Stuttgart, but nothing came to me. Luckily Shirley, one of the Revelles, a three-piece vocal group we'd shared the bill with earlier in the night, noticed the pickle I was in. She got up from the table beside ours and came to the counter. "Can I help you there, honey? You seem to be havin' some trouble with the lingo. After five or six years of touring this place, I can *sprechen* a little *Deutsche*. Tell me what you want and I'll order for you."

I told her my order and asked her if she'd have a drink herself. She looked me up and down and smirked. "Sure, honey, I'll have a *screwdriver*, if your pocket's up to it."

I glanced back at her colleagues. "Maybe I should get drinks for them, too?"

Shirley shook her head. "They've had enough as it is. Anyway, Martha

105

Lee's got a bottle in her handbag. Even though this is only a three-star hotel, the prices they charge for drink here are outrageous." She touched my chin with one of her long false fingernails. "You go back and sit with the others, and I'll get Fritz here to bring the drinks over."

Back at our table, Trench, Hearn, Billy and Jay were laughing at something one of the other girls had said. Billy swallowed some beer and glanced at me. "Miranda was just telling us about what their hometown Detroit's like."

I took my seat. "Motor City!"

Miranda raised her double chin and pouted her big rouged mouth at me. "Motor City my ass. More like Bitch City, if you ask me. I never said we come from there, by the way. We just gravitated there some years back to try and make our name, like a million others."

Trench swallowed some whisky and looked at me. "The girls were saying there's nothing but rivalry, crooked deals and back-stabbing goes on there, even among their own black brothers and sisters."

Martha Lee – the largest member of the trio – raised her fan-like false eyelashes and shot Trench a fiery look. "Honey, don't come on with that black brother and sister shit like you was one of our kind. I know what you're after, cock sucker!"

Miranda patted the straight hair of her blond wig and broke into a hoarse laugh. "You tell 'im, sister! You tell 'im!"

Trench put his glass down and shook his head. "No, no, I wasn't trying to insult you; I was just repeating something I heard you say yourself earlier, that's all. I didn't mean any offence by it."

Martha Lee drew a deep breath – inflating her large breasts till they almost popped out over the top of her low frilly blouse – and broke into a fit of laughter. "Shit, the man's takin' me seriously again. And he's supposed to be your manager, boys! He has no savvy, that's for sure. The best that can be said for him is that he's got a pretty face, like James Dean in *Rebel Without a Cause*."

Miranda's eyes widened. "That's it! I was tryin' to think who he reminded me of all night, and you've put your finger on it right there. James Dean's the man."

Martha Lee looked at Trench. "Only this man's not quite as innocent or pretty, is he?"

Trench let his cigarette dangle from his mouth and slouched his shoulder. "You're not the first to notice the Dean resemblance, actually."

Miranda slapped her wide thigh. "Shit, look what you've gone done now, Martha Lee. The man's head's swellin' up like a pumpkin. There'll be no stoppin' his tongue now."

Martha Lee drained her glass and started fidgeting at a bottle cap protruding from her leopard-skin handbag. "As long as that's all that's swellin' up, I don't mind, sister."

Miranda guffawed while Martha Lee glanced up towards the bar to see if the barman was looking; then she poured gin into her glass. After she put the bottle back in her bag, she sat back in her chair and started patting her wig.

Shirley arrived at our table accompanied by the barman, who placed a tray of drinks in front of me. I stood up to pay him. When I sat down again, I found Shirley sitting in a chair beside me. I thanked her for getting me out of the scrape up at the bar and offered her a cigarette. While I was holding the lighted match out to her, she ran her pink tongue along her fat upper lip before inserting the filter tip in her mouth. Light from the flame twinkled in her chocolate-coloured eyes as the golden tobacco grains turned red. She puffed a plume of smoke playfully in my face and then sat back and stretched out her bare knees till one of them touched my leg. She looked at me, sipping her screwdriver. "I meant to say it to you back at the club earlier, you've got a hellava voice for a white boy. Martha Lee and me was listening to you at the side of the stage before you came off. Where'd you learn to sing like that? If I hadn't had my eyes open, I'd have swore you was a blood brother."

I tried to control a slight tremor in my leg. "I've always liked black music. I guess the influence rubbed off over the years." I studied her dark features. She was easily the best looking of the three girls, but that wasn't saying much, as the other two were nothing to write home about. I turned to Hearn. "Peters and Mac must have gone to bed?"

Hearn glanced at Shirley's knee pressing against my leg. "Yeah, they went off while you were up at the bar."

Shirley flicked ash on the carpet. "Peters is your keyboard player, right? A fine musician. He and the rest of your band backed us real good tonight, and with only one quick rehearsal. You sure know your soul and Motown."

Martha Lee put some mixer in her gin and leaned forward. "One time we had our own full-time backing band on the road ten months a year. In the early sixties that was, when our single, 'Too Much Love In My Heart', was ridin' the charts back home."

I shook my head. "The name doesn't ring a bell. A bit before my time."

Trench leaned forward and widened his eyes. "What was the title again?"

Martha Lee straightened up. " 'Too Much Love In My Heart'. Came out in '63. Got some great notices in the press."

Trench shook his head. "No. I think I remember a number called 'Too Much Love' all right, but it didn't have the 'In My Heart' bit at the end."

Miranda stuck out her chest and patted her wig. "It reached number 31 in *Billboard*. It was playlisted on all the big stations at the time."

Trench ran his fingers through his hair. "Sing a bit of it. It might come back to me."

Miranda turned to Shirley. "You sing it, Shirl. She did the lead."

We all looked at Shirley. It was impossible to say if she was blushing, but her eyelashes started fluttering. She gulped back some screwdriver and took a deep breath. *"I've been all alone since you went. You, my all, my heaven-sent. What can I do without you? I feel so desperately blue."* She paused while Miranda tapped her foot four times on the floor; then the three of them raised their chins and pitched for the chorus: *"Too much love in my heart. I feel so torn apart. Too much pain in this strain. Can't get my man back again. . ."*

When the song came to an end, we broke into a spontaneous round of applause. Two other hotel guests sitting in a shadowy corner close by started clapping as well. Trench got to his feet and beckoned to the barman, making circular movements around the two tables with his outstretched finger. "Drinka all rounda, *bitte*."

Shirley did some more interpreting and the barman brought a large round of drinks to the tables.

Trench proposed a toast. "To one of the finest female groups we've ever had the pleasure to work with."

Martha Lee sniggered. "The man's bullshittin' again. I bet we's the first female group you ever shared the bill with anywhere. Am I right?"

I shook my head. "No, actually. We backed a trio of girl singers in a club in Birmingham just before we came over here. The Florets they were called."

Hearn laughed. "The three of them were like Dusty Springfield looka-likes. They had the beehive hairdos and tight sequinned dresses, the lot. The only thing that wasn't like Dusty was their singing. They were pure parrots. When Johnny introduced them on stage after our opening set, he made a right balls of it. Forgot their name and ended up announcing them as the Whatchamaycallems."

Everyone laughed. I swallowed some beer and laughed, too, even though I felt a right fool. "I didn't do it deliberately. I got confused because I couldn't find the piece of paper with their name."

Jay put down his glass. "I was as embarrassed as hell counting them in. Their leader kept throwing dagger looks at us till the crowd started applauding after their first number."

Hearn glanced at Shirley. "It wasn't their singing the crowd liked. One of them was real stunner, the youngest one. Do you remember her, Johnny? You tried to get off with her after the gig."

Shirley looked at me. "After what you'd called them? You had some nerve."

I gave Hearn a sour look, knowing what he was up to.

Billy glanced at me and laughed. "Tell them what happened when you went to their dressing room, Johnny."

I lowered my eyes. "Nothing happened."

Hearn laughed. "That's not what you told us on the night."

I took up my glass and started drinking beer to try and cover up my embarrassment.

Billy laughed. "Nothing happened is right. When he went to try and chat your one up, he found the dressing room door open, and you'll never guess what he saw when he looked in?"

Billy became embarrassed and broke into a laugh. Hearn took up the story: "Two of the girls were locked in a passionate embrace, kissing and fondling one another, and one of them was the one Johnny fancied."

Miranda slapped her knee. "Shit, she was a dyke?! Poor boy. Must've been hard on you?"

I shrugged and tried to laugh. "A bit of an eye-opener all right."

Martha Lee looked at me. "What age are you, honey?"

I hesitated. "Seventeen."

Hearn laughed. "Only just." I glared at Hearn. "My birthday was almost three months ago, actually."

Shirley touched my hand and stared at Hearn. "Don't be teasin' the boy. He's sensitive. There's no sin in that."

Miranda looked at me. "You're gonna come across a lotta peculiar things in this business, honey. So you may as well get used to it."

Martha Lee nodded solemnly. "That is for sure!"

This turn in the conversation dampened the party spirits somewhat. Miranda and Martha Lee drifted into a private conversation, while the rest us sat bleary-eyed from the smoke swirling around our tired heads. Trench sat forward and raised his glass. "Hey, don't go falling asleep on me. We still have all these drinks to finish."

Martha Lee looked at her watch, drained her glass and stood up. "It's almost three o'clock. I've had more than my quota. I'm goin' to bed."

Miranda tottered to her feet. "Hold on, sister, and I'll be with you. We still have to put our order in for breakfast at reception."

Shirley put her cigarettes and lighter in her handbag and leaned over to me. "I have the new album by Smokey Robinson and the Miracles back in my room. You might like to come back and hear it, if you're not too tired."

My breath drained away. I glanced across the table to see if any of the boys had heard the invitation. None of them were looking our way.

"No, I'm not tired. That would be nice. I really like Smokey."

Shirley smiled. "Room 35. Don't come with me now or the others will start goading you. Come up a few minutes after I've gone. It's on the second floor. Don't forget the number now."

"Room 35. I won't forget."

As soon as she left the bar Hearn stared at me. "Well, what was she saying? I was watching you."

"You'd love to know, wouldn't you?"

Jay smirked. "Why don't you follow her up and give her what she's asking for?"

Billy rubbed his hands together. "Go on, hurry on or it'll be too late."

Trench laughed. "I bet he's still a virgin, aren't you, Johnny?"

I lit a cigarette and drank some beer without saying anything. The fellas continued teasing me for a few minutes, then changed the subject. When my cigarette was finished, I stubbed it out and got to my feet. My head was fuzzy. I staggered slightly moving away from the table. Hearn sneered at me. "You wouldn't have been able to perform with her anyway. You're pissed."

I took a deep breath and tried to hold myself straight. "Goodnight, lads. See you in the morning."

"Goodnight, Johnny."

On my way upstairs I began to feel nervous. At one point I stopped and thought of retracing my steps to my own room, but I kept going, taking deep breaths as I neared the second floor. When I reached room 35, I hesitated before knocking.

"Come in. It's open."

I stepped inside and found myself almost in total darkness, except for some amber street light coming through a gap in the curtains. Smokey Robinson's angelic voice was swirling in a high octave at low volume. In silhouette, Shirley beckoned to me from the centre of the double bed. "I'm over here, honey."

I took a breath and stepped towards the bed, becoming aware of a strong smell in the room. The closer I drew to Shirley, the stronger the smell became. I tried to figure out what it reminded me of, and the only thing I could think of was fish.

"Take off your jacket and shoes, if you like."

I took off my jacket and slipped out of my desert boots, then sat on the edge of the bed. Shirley put her arms around my neck and drew me back to the pillows. She was wearing a short silky slip with a frill round the neckline. We started kissing and fondling. I became aware that she wasn't wearing anything under the slip. I touched something wet. The fishy smell became almost overpowering. I became light-headed. Shirley's lips started sucking at my mouth. My shirt came off and then my trousers. I began to feel dizzy. The room started going into a spin. Shirley legs were wide open and she was pulling at my head. I took a deep breath and gripped on to her hips. I began to feel like I was being sucked into a dark whirlpool. Everything was going round and round. I clung on to her body and went with the flow. A sense of being swallowed up came over me, and my mind went blank.

The sound of movement in the room next door woke me at dawn. Shirley was fast asleep on the pillow beside me with just a sheet covering her body. I crept out of the bed and located my clothes and shoes. I dressed quickly and left the room. On my way down the hall, I tried to recall what had occured between Shirley and myself the night before, but all I could remember was the strong smell of fish.

SWINGING LONDON

A baby born in blood cries out as it should
For where there's life there's pain
IN THE AFTERBIRTH

I T WAS DARK when I arrived at the mother and child home in Swiss Cottage. A young nurse answered the door.

"Is there a Celia Quinn staying here?"

The nurse smiled. "Yes, I think I saw her in the TV lounge a while back. You can wait for her in the waiting room just down the hall. It'll be warm there. Who will I say's calling?"

I thought for a moment and smiled. "One of Granny's boys, tell her. I think she'll know who you mean. I'm a friend of her boyfriend."

In the waiting room, I leafed through a woman's magazine but couldn't concentrate on any of the articles. I'd only met Celia on three or four occasions, and each time in the company of her boyfriend Tom, who did most of the talking. All I could remember of Celia was her eyes, large and bright with a sprinkle of freckles beneath them.

The door opened and Celia stepped into the room wearing a blue dressing gown. She looked at me slightly bewildered, then smiled. "My God, it is you. When the nurse said 'One of Granny's boys', I thought it might be you. But then I said, No, what would he be doing here? You've taken the wind out of me. I'd better sit down."

I took the seat beside her, noticing a strong scent of talcum powder. "Tom got the number of a club I was playing in from a music paper and phoned me with the news. I couldn't believe it. I didn't even know you were pregnant."

Celia put her hand up to her neck, covering her partly exposed cleavage. "I suppose Tom put you under pressure to come?"

I shook my head. "No, no, he just told me about the baby, that's all. I wanted to come and see you myself. Is it a boy or a girl? Tom didn't say."

Celia smiled. "A boy. Nine pounds three ounces. He has Tom's stubby nose. But he's lovely. I'll take you down to see him in a few minutes. But first tell me, how've the band been getting on since you moved here? Tom never stops talking about you. He thinks you're really going to make the big time."

I rubbed my neck. "I don't know about that. But things have been going pretty good. We've been to Germany for a short tour, and we played at that big outdoor festival at Glastonbury recently. That really went great for us. All the big record companies had scouts at it, and a few of them approached our manager about signing a record deal. He's negotiating with two or three of them at the moment. But enough about me. Tom was saying you had a tough delivery?"

Celia squeezed her hands. "He has an awful mouth, that fella."

I looked into her eyes. They were still quite bright but not as clear as I remembered. Her face was thinner, too, and the freckles had all but disappeared from her cheeks. "He's just concerned about you, that's all. How bad was it?"

Celia ran her hand over her pinched face. "I'm fine now. The worst is over. There were complications during the delivery. I had to have a caesarean section; I didn't feel a thing, though. I was under an epidural. But it was still awful; the worry of wondering how it was all going to turn out. Then I developed blood poisoning when I started breast feeding. I was sick for a week; couldn't keep anything down."

I searched for something consoling to say. "You were great to get through it all on your own."

Celia smiled. "That was the hardest part. But the doctor was really nice and the nurses were great. The matron asked me to consider putting the child up for adoption, but I couldn't do that. He's a little dote. Wait till you see him."

"Do your family know?"

Celia's body stiffened. "That was part of the problem. I think the reason I had all the complications was because I was so run down and worried. I kept it a secret at home right up until the last few months."

"How'd you manage that?"

Her eyes hardened. "I starved myself to keep down my weight. I was hardly noticeable up until the last couple of months. I'm from down the country, Tipperary. I don't go home often, but when I do, the whole locality know about it. People around our place are very stiff about this kind of thing. And they're fierce gossips." She looked down at her hands. "My mother twigged it in the end. She has an eye like a hawk. She wasn't too bad about it, but when she told my father, he blew a fuse. He told me I was a disgrace to the family and insisted that I come over here to have the child. One of my brothers turned on me as well; he called me a whore. He came to my flat in Dublin and found Tom there. He tried to start a fight with him. But you know Tom, he wouldn't hurt a fly. I'll never forgive my brother."

I leaned forward. "He was probably just worried about you."

Celia's eyes started to water. "Maybe, but he had a cruel way of showing it."

I scratched my head, thinking that maybe I would have reacted the same way had Celia been my sister.

Celia took a paper hanky from her pocket and rubbed her eyes. "It's my mother I'm really worried about. She hasn't been well lately. Back problems. She had a disc put in a few years back but still suffers terrible pain. I hate having caused her this upset on top of everything else. I've written to her three times since I arrived here two weeks ago."

I rubbed my neck, trying to think how long it had been since I'd written to my mother. All I could recall was a postcard of Buckingham Palace sent almost two months before. "How about Tom? It's a wonder he didn't come over with you?"

Celia blew her nose. "He couldn't afford it. You know yourself how badly paid musicians are in Ireland. He helped pay my way, though. And he phones every other night. He has a heart of gold, Tom. I have no complaints about him."

I sat back. "Any chance of you tying the knot?"

Celia laughed. "You're very old fashioned. People don't automatically get married now when they have a baby, you know. He's offered, and I'm thinking about it. But I don't know how we'd survive on what he earns as a musician. He's offered to mind the baby during the day, if I go back to the civil service. But I don't think he realises the commitment necessary to looking after a child. Can you imagine Tom changing nappies and wheeling a buggy around Stephen's Green?"

I laughed. "What are you going to do, then?"

Celia hesitated. "I've asked Tom to consider giving up the band and getting a steady job. He used to be a teller in a bank before he got into the music business."

A picture of Tom on stage came into my head, waving his Fender around like Jimi Hendrix. I shook my head. "I can't imagine Tom giving up music. It would be hard on him."

Celia straightened up. "He keeps saying himself that his band are going nowhere. They've been on the road for nearly two years and they're still only doing support spots. They earn less than people on the dole. It would be different if he was in a successful band like yours."

I laughed. "Successful! Do you know what we had for dinner today? Leftovers from breakfast. One of the waitresses at the hotel we're staying at up in Lancaster Gate gives us extra sausages so that we can make sandwiches. Hearn often takes her out on a date; that's why she's so good to us."

Celia laughed and stood up. "Yeah, but you're going places. Come on, I'm dying to show you the baby. He's in a sleeping room just down the hall."

While we were making our way down a narrow corridor, two girls in bright dressing gowns came towards us. Celia smiled at them in passing. When they were out of earshot, she turned to me. "The one in yellow is only fifteen. Kitty's her name. She's from Kerry. She arrived only a few days ago. I'm sharing a room with her and two other girls. She bawled her eyes out all last night. We didn't get a wink of sleep with her, poor thing. She doesn't know what she's going to do with her baby yet. She's thinking of putting it up for adoption. The other girl's from Manchester. She was telling me the other night that this is her second child. She had an abortion the first time but couldn't go through with it again."

I glanced over my shoulder at the two girls. "You'd wonder how that can happen over here with contraceptives freely available."

Celia shook her head. "I was thinking the same thing when I was talking to her."

In the infants' room, a young mother sitting behind a row of Perspex cribs was breastfeeding a tiny child. I turned away so as not to embarrass her.

Celia leaned into one of the small transparent cribs and took out her baby bundled in a white crochet quilt. She kissed his forehead and spoke affectionately to him for a moment, then held him out to me. I reluctantly took the baby in my arms and looked down at the small pink face. His eyes opened for a moment and looked up at me. I held my breath. Through the fluffy fabric of the quilt, I could feel the gentle pulse of his breathing against my arm. I had held my brothers and sisters as infants in the past, but this felt different. Tom and Celia were roughly my own age. The thought that I might be capable of fathering such a child made me feel almost dizzy. "He's so tiny, like a doll. I'm afraid I'll let him fall. Here, you take him, to be on the safe side."

Celia took the child and cradled him in her arms for a few moments; then she put him back in the crib and touched his nose. "Do you not see the resemblance to Tom?"

I laughed. "God forbid. I think he has your eyes anyway. That should well compensate for the nose."

Celia smiled and lowered her chin.

"Have you decided what you're going to call him yet?"

"Frank, I think, after my father. I don't know how he'll take it. He told me before I left that I won't be welcome home till I get married." She tucked the quilt up around the child's chin, muttering baby talk. Then she led me out of the room. "Come on, we'll let him sleep. I want to show you something I have in my bag. It's in my room, just down the hall here."

The room we entered had four beds, two occupied by young women, one reading a magazine, the other sleeping. Celia's bed was by a tall window. While she was rooting around in her handbag, I sat on a chair beside a wooden locker. "How long have you been here?"

"This is my third week. By right I should have left almost a week ago, but the infection held things up." She took a coloured photograph from her bag and handed it to me. "Here it is. I took it a few months back outside the Flamingo Club, just before you and your band left for England. Remember?"

I looked at the snap. Tom and myself were standing beneath the neon Flamingo sign, my head just below the pink feathered tail of a very stilted-looking flamingo bird perched on top of the letter M. Tom had his arm around my shoulder, his long black hair covering his right eye.

I glanced at Celia. "He's a fine guitarist, Tom. He deserves to go far."

Celia raised an eyebrow. "We'll see."

I tried to hand the photograph back to her.

She shook her head. "No, no, you keep it. I'm sure Tom would like you to have it. I have the negative. I can have another print made up sometime."

A nurse came along and handed Celia a plastic tumbler of pink medicine. "Your tonic. How're you feeling this evening?"

"Fine, nurse. This is a friend from Ireland, Johnny. He's the singer with a famous band."

"Really."

I looked down at my shoes.

The nurse coughed. "And how is our famous Frank doing this evening?"

Celia swallowed the medicine and handed the tumbler back to the nurse. "He's sleeping now. I fed him just before Johnny arrived. He's grand."

"That's good."

The nurse moved on to the next bed. Celia glanced after her and put her hand over her mouth. "She's from Kilkenny. Most of the nurses here are Irish."

A trolley entered the room and came towards the beds. A woman in a check apron started pouring tea.

I stood up. "I'd better go and let you have your supper."

Celia got to her feet. "We only get a cup of tea at this time. But I think you should go anyway. It's getting late. You shouldn't be out in the underground after dark. It's dangerous. One of the nurses told me that she had her purse snatched one night on the Piccadilly Line. You need to be careful over here."

I laughed. "I've been on the tubes dozens of times over the past few months and nothing's ever happened to me. I'll be fine."

As we made our way out the hall, Celia put on an English accent. "What do you think of Swinging London, then?"

"It's great. We had a few days off a few weeks back and I walked all round it. It's massive. I love Hyde Park."

Celia smiled. "I didn't get to see much of it myself, but maybe we'll come back some day when you're famous."

I laughed. "Fat chance."

At the front door, Celia kissed me on the cheek. "Thanks a million for coming. It was really great to see a familiar face."

I touched her arm. "Take care of yourself. I'll probably see you back in Dublin sometime."

When I got on the tube at Swiss Cottage, I found myself sitting opposite a young girl with dark eyes and long wavy hair. I glanced at her bare knees and turned away. The tube rushed on through the loud underground tunnel and came to stop at St John's Wood. A few passengers got off the train and others got on. A middle-aged man in a bowler hat sat beside the young girl and started reading a newspaper. After the train took off, I noticed him glancing down at her legs. Though I had done the same thing only minutes before, I felt slightly repulsed. I glanced at the girl's small breasts and calculated that she was no more than fifteen. I looked out the window. The young girl from Kerry that I'd seen back in the mother and child home came into my head. I remembered Celia telling me how she had cried all the night before because she didn't know what she was going to do with her baby.

The train screeched on through the loud tunnel and started pulling into Baker Street. I looked across at the young girl and noticed a small birth mark at the side of her mouth. She spotted me looking at her and smiled. The train came to a jolting stop. For a moment I forgot where I was; then I jumped up remembering I had to change trains.

DAVE

If you're stuck you'd better give up
And go back to work, David Miller
THE STORY OF DAVID

ARRIVED AT the Madison Hotel at around four in the morning feeling out of sorts with myself, having just come from the bed of a girl I'd picked up at a gig earlier in the night. Though I was tired, I didn't feel like going straight to bed. I got myself a cup of tea from a machine in the lobby and went to the lounge. I wasn't expecting anyone to be there at that time of the morning, but when I opened the door a fella in a leather jacket looked up at me from one of the tatty armchairs.

"Another night bird, like myself. Playin' a gig, were you? I've seen you and your band round the hotel before, haven't I? The name's Dave. Dave Garrick."

Dave's northern accent was a little hard on the ear, but after four or five months of touring the UK with the band, I was getting good at interpreting the various British accents I came across. I took a chair near the door. "I'm Johnny. Yeah, we were playing at the Speakeasy. I think I've seen you before, too. We've been staying here on and off for the last few months. You're in a band yourself?"

Dave ran his fingers through his long greasy hair. "Yeah, a blues group.

121

C Blue we're called. C as in letter in alphabet, not ocean or sight. I always have to explain that to people. We're just back from a grotty working-man's club in Brixton, a bread-and-butter gig. It's hard gettin' work in good places like the Speakeasy. Your band must have the right contacts to get playin' there. A good agent, have you?"

I swallowed some tea. "Howard Hughes. He took us on after we got a recording deal a few months back."

Dave's eyes widened. "Howard Hughes! He's one of best agents in London. What company are you with?"

"Deram. A subsidiary of Decca."

Dave raised his eyebrows. "Deram Records! How'd you manage to get in with them, then?"

I sat forward. "We've been lucky, I guess. We got a spot on that big out-door festival at Glastonbury soon after we moved here from Ireland. All the big record companies had scouts at it, and a few of them approached us. We picked Deram because we liked some of the bands on the label."

Dave relit a half-smoked roll-up cigarette. "Some people have all the luck. We moved down here from Newcastle almost a year to the day, thinkin' we were going to become the next Bluesbreakers, but we still have nowt to show for it. I'm sick to my teeth of goin' 'ungry for the blues. I think I'd be better off goin' home and takin' up my old trade as plumber. At least then I'd have a few bob at weekends for fags and beer. Half the time down here we don't even have enough for our grub."

I sipped my tea. "We were in the same boat until we got the recording deal. In fact, we're still living pretty much hand-to-mouth as it is. Most of the advance money we got from Deram went on a new van and new musical equipment."

Dave sucked at his cigarette. "Yeah, but at least you're in with a chance now. What's your band called?"

I hesitated. "Granny's Intentions. We used to be just the Intentions, but we changed the name recently. I'm not used to it myself yet."

"Funny name. What kind of music do you play?"

"Soul mainly, but we do some folk as well. Tim Hardin, that type of stuff."

"Never heard of him. Is he one of those new flower people from San Francisco? I've no time for that kind of thing. . ."

A head suddenly came round the lounge door and smiled at us, then disappeared. Dave sat up in his chair. "You know who that was? Joe Cocker. Must have been playin' out of town tonight. He's been gettin' great reviews lately in the *NME* and *Melody Maker*."

I finished my tea and got to my feet. "It's late. I'd better go up. We have a meeting tomorrow with a record producer who's been trying to get us to write original songs. So far we haven't been able to come up with anything decent. He's going to give us a few pointers on how to go about it tomorrow. Goodnight. And good luck with whatever decision you make about your career."

Dave shrugged. "My mind's practically made up. I'll be packin' in the band at end of month unless a miracle happens and we get signed to one of the majors like yourselves. Goodnight."

On the way upstairs, I winced at the smell coming from the grubby orange carpet. In the bedroom, I got out of my clothes and into bed without turning on the light. I could hear Mac's deep breathing in the single bed across from me. I closed my eyes but couldn't sleep. I started thinking of the fella I'd just left down in the lounge. I began to wonder what I would do if I were in his dead-end position. I tried to picture myself returning home a complete failure. The thought of it made me shiver in the bed. A line of an old song my father used to sing came into my head: *Keep right on till the end of the road, keep right on till the end.* I smiled at the memory, then turned on my pillow and started drifting off into a peaceful sleep.

Mac woke me a little before eleven the next morning. "Come on, Johnny, we'll be late for breakfast."

While I was getting into my jeans, Mac glanced at me from the sink. "That was some gig last night! I couldn't believe it when Hendrix walked in. Wait till I write home and tell them I played before Jimi Hendrix. They'll never believe me."

I zipped up my fly. "I think I spotted him looking at you when you were doing one of your solos."

Mac laughed. "I hope I didn't hit any bummers. I was really shittin' myself."

As we entered the dining room, Jimmy Young was signing off on the radio with the Beatles' 'Eleanor Rigby'. The dining room was almost full to capacity with down-at-heel musicians like ourselves. Mac spotted Hearn and Jay sitting by a window. We joined them and ordered our usual fry. On the radio, Paul McCartney's thin voice rose in pitch: *All the lonely people, where do they all come from? All the lonely people, where do they all belong. . .*

Hearn bit into a sausage and grinned across the table at me. "You disappeared very quickly after the gig last night. Get your oats again, did you?"

I grinned. "Like to know, wouldn't you? Where are the others?"

Hearn looked up at the ceiling. "I called Peters, but he was still out cold when I left the room. And Casanova here tells me that Billy won't be coming down because they were at it again all night with the two Swedes in the room next to theirs. Jay claims he gave it to his one four times. Did you ever hear the likes?!"

Jay grinned. "Don't believe me if you don't want to."

I glanced at Jay's almost skeletal face and laughed. "What's four times to a muscle-man like him!"

Soon after our breakfasts arrived, Peters came into the dining room self-consciously yawning and rubbing his eyes. He pulled up a chair beside me and started readjusting his glasses. "I'll take a cup of your tea if you don't mind, Johnny? I'm late for breakfast. What time's Tony due? Was it two or three Trench said?"

"Three, I think." I looked at Hearn for confirmation.

Hearn swallowed some tea. "Between half two and three. Trench has already left to meet him. After their meeting at Deram, they're having lunch and then coming here. I wonder what advice he's going to give us."

Mac swallowed some food. "He's probably just going to tell us what he knows about putting songs together from how other people he's worked with do it."

Peters turned to me. "I got an idea for a song myself yesterday about a girl who talks to herself on the phone. I have a bit of it worked out but not enough to play it."

I looked across the dining room and spotted Dave, the musician I'd met the night before in the lounge. He was sitting at a table with two other long-haired fellas from his band. He smiled across at me. I nodded back at him and turned to Peters. "I think I might have stumbled on an idea for a song myself."

Hearn laughed. "I hope it's better than your last effort, 'Shadow Man'. I couldn't make head nor tail of what that was about."

A few days before, I had put together a half-baked song about a character who is haunted by his own shadow. I thought it was OK until I sang it to the band and they blanked it. "At least I've been trying to come up with something."

Peters looked at me. "What's the idea for the new one?"

I hesitated. "A failed musician returns to his hometown to take up his old job."

Hearn laughed. "What put that into your head? Could you not think of something more ballsey?"

Peters sipped his tea. "No, it's not a bad starting point. Lots of great songs are written about negative things. But what about making the failed musician a failed painter or a failed poet? That might make it a bit more original."

I rubbed my neck. "I'm not so sure about that."

Peters shrugged. "It was just a suggestion. We could try out a few ideas and see which one works best."

Mac sat up. "Why don't we take our instruments up to our room after breakfast and see what we can come up with? It would be great to have a song written for when Tony arrives."

Jay shook his head. "Count me out. I'm going back to bed after I finish this coffee. I know nothing about melody or words."

Hearn scratched his ear. "I'd be no good to you either. I was useless at English at school."

After breakfast, Peters and Mac got their instruments from our van, and the three of us went upstairs to Mac's and my room.

While the two boys were setting up their gear and getting in tune with one another, I sat on my bed with a writing pad, picking my brain for an idea. I thought about the conversation I'd had the night before with Dave and jotted down the first line that came into my head: *If you're stuck you'd better give up and go back to work, Dave.*

I said the words over a few times to memorise them and then sang the line to a simple melody that came into my head. Mac looked at me. "That's nice. Sing it again and I'll work out the chords."

While I was repeating the line, Peters played the melody on his organ and looked at me. "It's catchy all right, but the Dave at the end sounds stretched. Why don't you try using a full name, something like David Miller."

I sang the chorus using the name David Miller. Mac laughed. "That sounds great. Now all we need's a few verses and we're away in a hack."

We struggled with my idea of writing about a failed musician for a while without success; then Peters suggested turning David Miller into a failed poet and the lyric started taking off. As the verses developed, I lost more and more control of the direction the song was taking, till eventually David Miller ended up being more a reflection of Peters' character than mine. I resented this and began to feel the first pangs of artistic jealousy taking me over. In the end, however, I was glad when we managed to complete the full song.

> David Miller was a clerk and he looked the part
> He wrote poetry he thought was good
> Poetry that only he understood
> His nine-to-five existence left him cold
> He broke the hold
> Thumb your nose at convention
> It will cost you your pension
> But you'll manage, David Miller
> Oh, the freedom was fine but he wasted his time
> Now his writing hours are all disarranged
> With so many things to do, his small savings flew
> Poetry is strange at the labour exchange
> And his hair grew long and he stood out in the throng
> All his friends said he had the knack
> Many fools were impressed by the way that he dressed
> But the publishers laughed and sent his poems back
> If you're stuck you'd better give up and go back to work
> David Miller.

THE LAUNCH

I sold my soul to be a winner
ON THE WATER

'D WASHED MY hair for the fourth time since having it permed the day before, but still my head was a mass of fuzzy curls. I cursed myself in the mirror above the sink and ran a comb through my fringe in a useless attempt to straighten it out. "How the hell did we ever let Peters talk us into getting this done?"

Mac glanced at me from a chair beside his bed. He had the same permed style as me, only his didn't look quite as fuzzy. He ran his fingers through his curls and smiled. "I'm kind of getting used to it. Clapton had his done like this recently. It's all the go."

I raised my eyebrows. "Yeah, but six of us all with the same style!"

Mac sat up. "It's the stage outfits we're going to be wearing that I don't like. When we tried them on at the fitting the other day, I felt like one of Robin Hood's merry men. I didn't want to say it in front of Peters after all the thought he put into designing the gear, but I think they're a big mistake."

I gave up on my hair and flopped on to my bed. "Your outfits aren't as bad as mine. My shirt has pleated sleeves and a frill down the front, for Christ sake. I feel like King Henry VIII in it. It's ridiculous! We should never have listened to those PR pricks at Deram when they suggested that we go for a uniform look."

Mac sat back. "The idea was OK. It's what Peters did with it that's the problem."

A loud knock came to the door. Mac opened it. Hearn came in puffing a cigarette. "The van's leaving in two minutes. We have to pick up the outfits at Carnaby Street and get to the hotel before the press arrive. The reception starts at half three, remember? Let's go, Curly Joe."

I looked at Hearn's fuzzy hair. "Look who's calling who Curly Joe!"

During the drive downtown, Trench started laughing behind the wheel. "I can't help it, lads. I feel a bit like Noddy driving a group of gollywogs to a tea party."

When we reached Carnaby Street, Peters and Hearn went into the boutique and returned to the van laden down with our handmade stage outfits. While they were placing them in the back, Hearn started shaking his head. "I hope we don't get jeered off the stage in this gear. It really is outlandish."

Peters kept a straight face. "We won't, don't worry."

When we arrived at the hotel, we had to haul our musical equipment up two flights of stairs to the reception room. While we were setting the gear up on stage, caterers in white uniforms were busy laying out buffet food on a long white table at one side of the floor. We ran through the A and B sides of our single a couple of times and went to our dressing room as the first members of press corps were beginning to arrive.

While we were getting into our stage outfits, Jay started laughing. "Will you look at Peters! He looks like an old granny in those puffy sleeves with the glasses and the frizzy hair."

Billy chuckled. "Isn't that what we're supposed to be – old grannies?"

I looked down at my pink pleats and cursed. "I don't know what you think's so funny. We look like a bunch of morons, if you ask me. What the hell are we doing at all? I though we were supposed to be a rock band. We've really sold out!"

Jay gave me a puzzled look. "What's up with you? We're in show-business, aren't we?"

"Speak for yourself!"

Peters looked at me over the rims of his glasses. "How come you waited to make your objection till now, Johnny?"

"You didn't ask for my opinion before this, did you?"

Peters shrugged. "You have a mouth, haven't you? And a big one, too, when you want to get your own ideas across. You're just jealous because you didn't think of this yourself."

I looked down at my frills and laughed. "Jealous? Of this? You must be joking!"

Peters shook his head and started squinting. "You're a right prick, Johnny, do you know that?"

I jumped at Peters and gripped him by the throat. His glasses fell on the floor. Hearn pounced on my back and started pulling me away. Billy and Jay grabbed Peters and held him back. At that moment, Trench came into the room with a tray of glasses and a bottle of champagne. "What the hell's going on here?!"

I stood by the row of wardrobes breathing heavily. Hearn loosened his grip on my shoulders and stepped away from me. "It's nothing, just a bit of tension, that's all. Johnny's nervous. We're all nervous."

Peters picked up his glasses and stood by a mirror examining his throat. "He tried to choke me!"

Trench put the tray on a table and stared at me. "What's gotten into you, Johnny?"

"Nothing. I just feel like a stooge in these clothes, that's all."

Hearn grinned. "Yesterday you said you felt like Harpo Marx. Make up your mind, will you."

Trench moved to the middle of the room. "Listen, we didn't burst our balls over the last six months trying to get this break so that you can blow it now. There are dozens of top people from the music press waiting to pass judgement on you out there. For Christ sake, forget about what your wearing. It's too late to do anything about that now. Anyway, I think you look great. Come on, Johnny, shake hands with Peters and apologise."

I took a deep breath and held my hand out towards Peters. "I'm sorry."

Peters took a hesitant step towards me and shook my hand without saying a word.

Trench started pouring champagne. "Come on now, have one drink before you go on stage. It'll loosen you up. Then get out there and knock them dead. Remember, you have only the two songs to play, so get into it straightaway."

Deram's MD introduced the band on stage. I felt deeply embarrassed stepping up to the main microphone. Cameras flashed in my face as the band launched into the B side of our single, 'Sandy's on the Phone'. While I was singing, I noticed a fella wearing sunglasses at the front of the stage sneering up at me, but at the end of the song there was a loud round of applause.

Because our producer had used a number of studio effects in the recording of 'The Story of David', we didn't perform it nearly as well as the recorded version. Still, when we brought it to a close, there was another loud round of applause.

The moment we came off stage, I rushed back to the dressing room and changed into my ordinary clothes. When I returned to the hall, our single was playing over the PA system at low volume. I joined a queue at the buffet table and got some food and a glass of wine.

While I was eating, Trench came along and introduced me to a journalist with a pimply face. The journalist sipped a glass of white wine and looked at me. "I was just saying to your manager, I love your image. So many bands nowadays don't care about their stage appearance."

I waited for him to comment on our single. He drank back some more wine and licked his lips. "Excellent Chardonnay. Deram really know how to splash out, don't they?"

Trench grinned. "Yeah, when other people are paying the bill."

The journalist laughed. "Oh, yes, I see what you mean."

I drained my glass and retreated to the table for a refill.

Deram's MD came up behind me and put his hand on my shoulder. "That was quite a performance, Johnny. Everyone's talking about your image. You must be pleased?"

A fella wearing sunglasses approached me with a grin on his face. "I didn't know you there for a moment without your frills."

I recognised him as being the character who had sniggered at me while I was on stage. I ignored him and turned back to the MD, but he was gone. The fella in the sunglasses stood in front of me. "I'm not trying to goad you, man. I thought your voice was terrific and your first song was really nice."

I took a sip of wine. "Thanks. I'll pass on the compliment to our keyboard player. He wrote it."

The fella readjusted his sunglasses and started to walk away. "By the way, I write for *NME.*"

Time went by. The crowd became more noisy. I spotted Peters having a head-to-head conversation with Trench near the stage. I went up to them and told Peters what the journalist from the *NME* had said about his song. He was delighted. He apologised for the row we'd had earlier. Then he looked at Trench and started squinting. "Tell him what the guy from *Melody Maker* said."

Trench rubbed his neck. "I can't remember his name, but he really liked the single and told me to watch out for a review in next week's edition. His only criticism was that he thought Hearn looked a bit of a spare on stage."

I frowned. "What did he mean?"

Trench hesitated. "He thought he looked awkward doing nothing. But he's not the first person who's said that."

I took a breath. "But he sings, doesn't he?"

Trench lit a cigarette. "Mostly only backing singing now."

Peters rubbed his jaw. "He distracts attention from you, Johnny."

"I don't mind."

Peters cleared his throat. "That's not the point. From now on you're going to be singing all the important songs. It has to be like that. You have the best voice and the best image."

I remained silent for a moment, then I looked at Peters. "I'm not going along with this! We can't stab Hearn in the back the way we stabbed Alfredo. It wouldn't be right."

Peters looked away.

Trench took a deep pull from his cigarette. "No one's going to stab any-one in the back. We're simply going to explain the situation to Hearn and leave it up to him what to do."

Peters scratched his head. "I think Hearn knows the situation himself. Don't you remember how awkward things got for him in the studio when Tony chose you to sing the B side as well as the A side?"

Before I had a chance to answer, Deram's top PR man came towards me and raised my arm in the air. "I want to make a toast. To the finest singer on Deram's books! And remember, I'm the one who spotted you. Cheers!"

The reception broke up at around eight. A couple of hours after we returned to the hotel, a knock came to our room door. Mac opened it. Trench, Peters and Hearn came in. Hearn had a smile on his face but his shoulders were slouched.

He sat at the end of my bed and looked at me. "I have something important to tell ye. I've decided to leave the band. I've been thinking about it now for a while. Ye don't need two singers any more. And I'm gettin' a bit tired of being on the road, anyway."

I shook my head. "You don't have to do this, Hearn."

Hearn stood up. "I want to, I swear."

I looked at Peters and Trench, then turned back at Hearn. "This isn't right. We started out together. And now things are just beginning to go well. It isn't fair."

Hearn gave a forced laugh. "Don't worry, I'll be still rootin' for you all the way."

Trench stepped forward. "Yeah, and if the band hit the big time, we won't forget you."

Hearn laughed. "I'll hold you to that!"

I looked at Hearn and turned away. Conflicting emotions welled up inside me; sorrow for Hearn's situation but gladness also that the spotlight would now fall more directly on me, alone. Hearn stood in silence for a moment; then he ran his fingers through his curly hair and grinned at Peters. "My only regret is that I didn't come to this decision yesterday before we got our hair done."

"I Just Want Us to Go On Having a Bit of Fun, That's All"

I've often been under, I've often been down
MY FATHER WAS A SAILOR

M Y HEAD WAS pounding and my stomach felt raw and empty when I woke. The light coming through the curtainless window beside the bed was grey and dull and made the small bedsit look even bleaker than it normally looked. As I lay on my pillow listening to the faint sound of Mac snoring beside me, I began to recall bits and pieces of the night before. Maggie, an Irish prostitute, and her Jamaican husband Bob, a taxi-driver cum petty drug-peddler, had invited us upstairs to their room to listen to some ska and reggae records; and I had made a complete pig of myself by accepting every drink, joint and pill that had been offered to me. It had been well after three in the morning when we'd stumbled down to bed. Still, I couldn't go back to sleep now because of a gnawing emptiness in my stomach, which was due mainly to the fact that I had eaten very little the day before.

Though the band had no engagements that day or gig that night (after three flop singles in a row, gigs and engagements were few and far between), I slipped out of bed, got dressed and went to the kitchen, which we shared with a number of other tenants in the house. The cupboard where we stored our food was empty except for a bowl of sugar and a half bag of oatmeal. I took a pot from the press and milk from the fridge and made some porridge.

While I was eating at the Formica table, I heard footsteps approaching the kitchen. I thought it was Mac but it turned out to be Frieda, a German girl who lived in the room next to ours. She came into the kitchen in a faded Japanese dressing gown with a baby's milk bottle in her hand. When she saw me, she scratched her head and yawned. "Good morning. Having porridge again, I see. You'll turn into one of the three bears if you're not careful."

I laughed. "Or Goldilocks, perhaps."

Frieda went to the fridge and started filling the child's bottle with milk. "You made a lot of noise last night. Nearly woke Brigitte on me. You were up with Maggie and that man of hers again, yes?"

Frieda was a close friend of Maggie's. They worked the same night trade together, but Frieda had no time for Bob.

"They invited us up to listen to some music. I'm sorry about the racket we made. I fell coming down the stairs. I was a little drunk. How's Brigitte?"

"She's fine. She's used to noise with all my late-night comings and goings. But she's been a little unsettled with the changing babysitters since Rick went."

Rick was Frieda's partner (almost half her age, according to Maggie). He had walked out on her a few weeks earlier. On the day he left, Frieda took an overdose of pills. Maggie found her lying on the floor of her room and came knocking on our door, asking us to phone for an ambulance.

"Maggie was telling us last night that you're thinking of returning to Germany?"

Frieda tightened the belt of her dressing gown. "Maybe. My family there disowned me because of the work I do, so I'm not sure. I'm thinking about it. I have a sister who writes to me. She keeps asking me to go back, but I haven't been there in nearly ten years. I'm not sure if I'd be able to settle there now."

"Ten years is a long time all right."

"Maybe too long."

Frieda went to the sink and let the tap run over the child's bottle; then she started to leave the kitchen. When she reached the door she turned and smiled. "By the way, I meant to tell you yesterday, I heard your song on the radio again the other day, but it was the other band, not you, who was singing. I prefer your version. How is it doing for you?"

"OK."

This was a lie. The song Frieda was talking about, 'Never an Ordinary Thing', was a light-weight pop song that the band had reluctantly recorded a couple of months earlier when morale was at an all time low after 'The Story of David' and another single had failed to take off. We'd been given the new song by a commercial songwriting team who had a track record of hits behind them. Shortly after we brought it out as a single, a second version of the song was released by another band, causing a division of airplay which lessened the chances of either of the records getting into the charts.

"If you get on 'Top of the Pops' maybe you'll get Maggie and me tickets to go and see you, if we're not too old?"

"Fat chance."

After Frieda left the kitchen, I finished my porridge and headed out for my morning walk. When I returned to the bedsit an hour later, Mac was up and playing his guitar along with an Andres Segovia album of Bach airs. (By now Mac had become quite an accomplished musician, and his musical tastes were begging to branch out to classical music.) When he spotted me, he put down the guitar and lowered the volume of the record. "That was some night last night. I still have a pain in my head, and I didn't take half as much stuff as you. You must be feeling rotten altogether?"

I sat on a chair. "I was when I woke up, but I'm not too bad now after my walk. I wish we had some money, though. I'd love to go to the pictures tonight. I'm sick of being cooped up in this kip all the time."

Mac scratched his ear. "It's a good meal I'd like. But at least we have a gig tomorrow night. We'll have a little money then."

I glanced round the bare room. "Maybe we'll walk over to Billy's and Jay's place later to watch TV?"

"Good idea."

I stood up. "How about teaching me another few chords on the guitar now?"

Mac handed me his guitar. "OK, but I don't want to hear any more about sore fingers. If you want to learn how to play the guitar, you'll have to put up with the pain."

We headed out for Billy's and Jay's place in Lancaster Gate at around six in the evening. It was dark by the time we got there. Jay answered the intercom and let us in. Upstairs we ran into Billy coming from the toilet. The moment I looked at his eyes I knew he was stoned. "What are you on, Billy?"

Billy grinned. "Bennies. We got a whole load of them last night from a guy who lives upstairs in exchange for a small bit of hash. You can have a few, if you like. Come on in."

Billy led the way into his and Jay's dimly lit bedsit. As usual, the place was a mess, with clothes, magazines and record sleeves scattered all over the beds and chairs. The TV was off. A Marvin Gaye album was playing at loud volume on Billy's old mono record player.

From an armchair in front of a small electric fire, Jay raised a can of cider. "Pull up a chair and make yourselves at home, lads. We're on the last can, but we have lots of Bennies. We haven't been to bed for two days, but we still feel great, don't we, Billy?"

Billy rubbed his eyes and coughed. "Yeah, but I think we'll take another few Bennies with the boys, just to keep topped up."

Jay sat up in his chair. "Good idea. I was beginning to feel a little drowsy there a minute ago. I could do with a bit of a lift."

While Mac and myself were settling in around the electric fire, Billy took some pills from a brown envelope and handed them to us. "Give them the can there, Jay, so they can wash them down. And here's another couple for you."

We passed around the cider and swallowed the pills, then sat back and started chatting about gigs we'd played in the past. Billy and Jay did most of the talking at first, but eventually the Benzedrine began to loosen Mac's tongue as well. He looked at me and laughed. "Remember that club we played in Belfast? There were riots just down the street from the venue. Paisley was out with his mob."

I widened my eyes. "Oh, yeah, I remember that one all right. Someone had to escort us by a safe route back to our B&B after the show. The thing that stuck in my mind most about that gig was that Van Morrison was at it.

Remember? One of the bouncers kicked him out of the club at the end of the night because he wasn't with any of the bands."

Jay looked at me. "*The* Van Morrison. From Them?"

I nodded. "Them had just broken up at the time. Van told us that he was thinking of going to America."

Billy laughed. "And to think what's become of him since."

A couple of hours went by. We took some more pills and washed them down with strong coffee. A little after midnight, the people next door started pounding on the wall because of the music. Billy hopped up and gave the two finger salute to the wall but turned down the record player a little. Mac and myself got to our feet, ready to leave, but Jay persuaded us to stay. "You can kip here for the night. I think you've missed the last tube anyway."

Just before three in the morning, Billy nodded off on the arm of his chair and started snoring. Jay tried to wake him by shaking his shoulder, but it was pointless. After two days without sleep, he had run out of steam. Jay took a pill from the envelope and tried to force it into Billy's mouth. Mac hopped up and pushed Jay's hand away, knocking the pill on to the floor. "What the hell are you trying to do? You could kill him!"

Jay got down on his hands and knees and started searching for the pill under the chairs. "What did you do that for? That was one of the last ones we had."

I watched Jay groping around on the rug in front of the electric fire. "Leave it, Jay! We've had enough. It's time to go to bed anyway. We have a gig tomorrow night, remember?"

Jay looked up at me, bleary eyed. "I just want us to go on having a bit of fun, that's all."

Mac and myself put the two boys to bed; then we bedded down ourselves on some cushions on the floor. With the Benzedrine still active in our systems, we found it hard to sleep. We tossed around for hours, listening to Jay and Billy snoring in their beds. The sun was coming through the curtains when I finally managed to nod off.

The persistent sound of the doorbell ringing woke me a few hours later. None of the others showed any sign of answering it, so I forced myself over to the intercom. I pressed the button. Peters' voice boomed in my ear. "Open up, for Christ sake. I've been ringing here for the past five minutes! I have something important to tell you."

As he entered the room, Peters pegged his nose. "Phew! What's been going on here?!"

Billy's head surfaced from his pillow. "Don't tell me it's time to go to the gig already?"

Peters laughed. "It's not even noon yet. What were you on, Billy?"

Billy groaned. "Mind your own business. Just because you want to live like a saint doesn't mean we all have to. What's up? We didn't get to bed till the crack of dawn. We're knackered."

Peters looked at Billy over the rims of his glasses. "If you don't want to hear the good news I've got, I'll hold it till later."

Mac sat up on the floor. "What good news?"

Peters took a step towards the door. "I'll tell you on the way to the gig in the afternoon. The lads don't want to hear it now."

I looked at Peters. "For Christ sake, stop prickin' around and tell us the news."

Peters turned round. "Trench phoned my place from Dublin an hour ago to tell me that 'Never an Ordinary Thing' has just gone into the Irish top ten at number seven. Larry Gogan has been raving about it on his radio show for the past couple of weeks, and Terry Wogan has given it a great review in the *RTÉ Guide*. We'll be flying home in a couple of weeks to do 'The Late Late Show' and to start a nationwide tour of the big ballrooms. Our photograph's already splashed all over the Irish papers. We're famous."

The Old House

There is a time in life, it seems,
For believing in dreams
THERE IS A TIME

"THE BACKS OF people's houses can be far more revealing than their fronts. Take that one, for instance. The front of that house is impeccable. Pure white. I know it well. I pass it every day on my way to school on the bus. But look at that for a mess!"

I wasn't quite sure what to make of Helen's observation about the back of the house we were looking at, so rather than say something stupid I put my arm around her and kissed her. "You're a strange fish, do you know that? Now I see why you like strolling in back alleys and laneways. You're a bit of a snoop."

Helen laughed. "I am not. I just like exploring areas that other people ignore, that's all."

We walked on. A white cat ran across the lane in front of us and scaled a red-brick wall. Helen smiled. "I hope white cats don't mean the opposite to black ones."

I took her hand and squeezed it. "I've never felt luckier in my life."

Helen flicked some hair out of her eyes. "I was thinking, if you're free on Saturday morning we could go to the Municipal Gallery again, and later I can get you that book of short stories I was telling you about by Franz Kafka in Eason's, seeing as you liked *The Castle* so much."

I rubbed my eye. "Before I met you, I thought all this arty stuff was for the birds. How did you get interested in it?"

Helen hesitated. "I was going out with this fella, an art student. He started lending me books and taking me to theatres and galleries. I knew nothing about the arts then. I felt like a real ignoramus. Then I started buying books and learning things for myself."

"You must have really liked the fella to go to all that trouble. Where's he now?"

Helen shrugged. "We broke up a few months back. But I didn't do it just for him."

I rubbed my neck. "I must admit that the only reason I started reading *The Castle* was because you gave it to me. I was too embarrassed to say it to you before, but that was the first book I ever read from cover to cover."

Helen's eyes widened. "Really?"

"I swear. I found it tough going at first, but I couldn't let it down in the end. You've opened up a whole new world for me, and I've only known you a few weeks."

Helen laughed. "What about Saturday, then? Will we go to the Municipal?"

I drew a breath. "I'd love to, but the band are down the country all weekend. I'll be free on Monday, though. Maybe we can meet then, when you finish school?"

Helen shook her head. "From next week on I'll be studying hard for my exams. It's getting very close. If I pass with more than three honours, my father's promised to buy me a second-hand car. We'll be able to go for drives together then."

"I thought you needed to be eighteen before you can get a license."

Helen looked at me. "I'll be eighteen by then. My birthday's in a few months' time. What age are you, by the way?"

I hesitated. "I won't be eighteen till next March."

Helen grinned. "How does it feel going out with an older woman?"

"You're not the first."

"I'll bet."

I leaned over and brushed back a strand of hair from her eye. "When am I going to see you, if we can't meet on Monday?"

Helen thought for a moment. "You could come to the house on Monday for tea, if you like. I think my mother likes you."

"If that's the only way I can get to see you, OK. Maybe you'll take me up to your room again and show me more of your things."

I had already been to Helen's house once before. We bumped into her mother briefly in the front garden pruning roses in the sun. There had been one slightly awkward moment for me when Helen announced that she was taking me up to her bedroom to show me her art books. But this didn't knock a feather out of her mother. She just smiled and told Helen not to keep me all day locked up in her stuffy room on such a glorious afternoon.

We emerged from the lane, crossed a street and entered another alleyway. Instead of the usual rows of sheds and garages that lined the sides of the other lanes we'd passed through, there were a few small two-storey houses in this one, all of them dilapidated and uninhabited. We stopped at one and looked through a broken window. Inside there was no furniture, just a scattering of old newspapers on a dusty floor. Helen moved over to the front door and tried to push it in. It opened slightly but then jammed, held by some obstacle from inside. I put my shoulder to it and pressed more firmly. It started to open. There was a table behind it, which I managed to shift back far enough for us to get in.

The small hallway was clouded with dust, and there were cobwebs everywhere. In the living room, Helen picked up one of the old newspapers from the floor. It was a faded copy of the *Irish Independent* dated June 1962. She read a few lines from one of the leading articles and then dropped the paper back on the floor.

We went upstairs, treading the wooden steps carefully as some of them were loose and rotting.

In the upper part of the house, there were two empty bedrooms, not quite as damp as the downstairs rooms. In the larger of these, Helen found a couple of faded photographs lying on a dusty shelf: one of an infant in what appeared to be a baptismal gown, the other of a young couple standing close together in stiff, old-fashioned clothes of the forties or fifties.

Helen brushed some flecks of dust from the woman's face. "A honeymoon photograph, I'd say. You can tell by the way they're dressed. People back then only had photographs taken for special occasions."

I took a second look at the young couple. "They seem happy together, don't they?"

Helen raised her eyebrows. "She does. He's a bit stiff looking."

"Maybe he was having second thoughts."

Helen smiled and looked at the other photograph. "I wonder was the baby theirs?"

"It's hard to say. All babies look so alike."

Helen shook her head. "No, they don't. They're all totally different. I think this little one's a bit like the woman. Look at their eyes."

I moved nearer to Helen and looked at the photograph more closely. I could see no resemblance between the woman and child, but I went on looking at their faces.

A delicate scent of flowers from Helen's neck replaced the damp, musty smell of the room. The rhythm of her breathing grew slightly uneven. She looked at me and her lower lip quivered. "They probably lived here together."

"Probably."

I looked around the bare room. Bright patches on the faded wallpaper showed where pictures had once hung and furniture had once stood. On the wall facing us, the curved outline of the head of a bed was clearly visible, with some faint oily head-marks on the wallpaper above it. Helen noticed this at the same time as I did. She looked at me and smiled. I took her hand and led her across to where the bed had once stood. I took off my jacket and spread it out on the dusty floor. The two of us lay down on it and started kissing.

The floorboards started creaking beneath us. Our eyes opened. Helen smiled. I noticed a tiny network of blue veins just below the arch of her eyebrow. I touched them and looked into her eyes. Her brown irises started dilating like two small sea creatures. I leaned down and kissed her eyes shut. Our mouths came together. Our tongues touched. I ran my hand over her hip and raised my knee to get closer to her. The wooden boards creaked again. We went on kissing.

When we got to our feet, we were both covered in dust. Helen picked up my jacket and shook it, then handed it to me. "I hope you didn't think me too prudish, but I don't want to become pregnant. It happened to a friend of mine recently, and I'm really frightened of it happening to me."

"I understand. It was lovely, anyway."

Helen bent down and picked up the two photographs from the floor and placed them back on the shelf where she'd found them. I leaned over and touched her face. "Why don't you take them with you as a memento?"

Helen shook her head. "No, no, they belong here. We can come back and see them again some other time, if you like?"

"That would be nice."

The sun was going down as we left the house. The sky was all pink and lavender with purple streaks running through it.

Helen was expected home early, so we made our way straight to the main road and caught a 47A bus to Donnybrook. We sat in the upper deck holding hands. A couple of young girls sitting a few seats in front of us started looking back in our direction. One of them whispered something to the other and then they both started giggling.

Helen smiled. "They'll be back for your autograph next."

"I hope not."

"How does it feel being famous?"

I laughed. "I'd hardly call a hit in the Irish charts fame."

"Your photograph's been on the cover of the *RTÉ Guide* and you've been on 'The Late Late Show'. You're a celebrity, admit it."

"Give over, will you?"

As we approached Donnybrook, Helen took a slim book of poetry from her handbag. "Before I forget it, here's an English translation of Bryan Merriman's *The Midnight Court*. It's quite a bawdy book. It was written by a Limerick man, like yourself. I think you'll like it."

"Why, because it's bawdy?"

"No, because you're from Limerick, silly."

I flicked through the pages. "It shouldn't take me as long to read as *The Castle*."

"I thought you liked *The Castle*?"

"I did. It reminded me of my own life in the music business."

Helen sat up. "What do you mean?"

"K's struggle to reach the castle is a bit like trying to reach the top in the music business."

Helen squeezed my hand. "But K never reaches the castle. At least you're successful now. I heard your song on the radio again this morning while I was having breakfast."

I looked out the window and noticed a man limping along the pavement on a pair of crutches. "I hate that song. I hate singing it on stage, and I cringe every time I hear it on the radio. We sold out when we recorded that. We were desperate at the time."

Helen looked at me. "But if you hadn't recorded it, you might never have come back to Ireland and we might never have met."

"True."

We got off the bus and walked the short distance to Helen's house.

We stood talking and kissing by her garden fence for ten or fifteen minutes; then Helen pulled away from me and looked at her watch. "I really have to go in now. My mother'll have a fit. Phone me tomorrow night. And I'll see you on Monday afternoon when you call for tea. Don't forget now!"

"How could I? Goodnight."

Rather than take the bus back to the hotel where the band were staying, I walked the two or three miles. On the way, I kept sniffing the front of my jacket for the sweet scent of Helen's perfume.

When I arrived at the hotel, I found Mac in our room, listening to the radio. He gave me a sour look as I closed the door. "Where the hell were you? Didn't you not know there was a band meeting this evening?"

"I got held up."

Mac shook his head. "There were sparks flying here earlier. Peters had a terrible row with Billy and Jay over the way they messed up the gig the other night when they went on stage out of their heads. He threatened to leave the band if they do it again. Billy told him to fuck off and walked out. Then Trench came round and there was another row, about our accounts. It seems there's going to be far less profit from the tour than we were expecting."

After my long evening with Helen, the last thing I wanted to do was discuss band business, but there was no escaping it.

"But we've been playing flat out since we got here over a month ago. Where's all the money gone?"

Mac hunched his shoulders. "Trench says we owe him for loans he advanced us over the past year and a half in England. He had all the facts and figures written out. Peters disputed a lot of it, but he got nowhere. He was cursing you for not being here to back him up."

"Where's he now?"

"Gone to town to meet his sister." Mac offered me a cigarette. "There's one other thing. The agency called from London with an offer of a month's residency in a club in Munich. The money isn't great, but Trench thinks we should take it. With our single dropping out of the Irish charts, he reckons it would be good to give the circuit here a rest for a while."

"When does the residency start?"

"In a few weeks."

Helen came into my mind. I lay back on my bed and looked up at a crack in the ceiling.

STRAY DOG

Was it by coincidence that we ended up
In a part of town so bleak and rough
Where the poor live in poverty
Was there a lesson there to be learned by me?
OUR LAST DRIVE

WAS WAITING by the window when Helen's mini pulled up under the amber street light outside my flat. I said a quick goodbye to Phil (a musician friend who was staying with me) and hurried out and got into the car. As we pulled away from the kerb, the vehicle jerked a few times. Helen cursed and drove off down Angelsea Road, glancing at me as she changed gears. "Where to tonight?"

I shrugged. "I'm easy. You decide."

Helen drew a loud breath. "You always say that and I hate it!"

"But it's true. I don't mind where we go as long as we're together."

Helen gave me a crooked look. "You're in a good mood for a change. What's happened?"

I glanced out the side window at an old woman raking leaves in a passing garden. "The band arranged another song of mine today with the new drummer and bass player, and it worked out really well. We almost have enough material to start recording the album now."

147

During the band's last English tour, we had passed on a demo of new songs to our producer, and, on the strength of them, he had committed himself to recording an album with us as soon as we had enough material of a similar standard put together.

"I suppose this means you'll be going away again soon?"

"We won't be gone that long, a month at the most. This is what I've always been aiming for, to record an album of original songs. And it's you I have to thank for it."

Helen glanced at me. "What do you mean?"

"Most of the songs are about you."

Helen shrugged. "You said that before, but I haven't heard any of them."

I rubbed my eye. "You'll hear them when we release them on record. By the way, I borrowed some lines from that book of poetry you gave me by Merriman for the new song. I hope no one notices."

"That's plagiarism."

"I didn't steal his ideas. I just used a few of his words to get my own lines moving. You're the one I was writing about."

"What words of his did you use?"

I rubbed my eye. "I can't remember exact words, but I put them in lines like *You're my comfort and delight. I'm haunted with thoughts of you at night. Oh, become my cheering light and make things seem bright.*"

Helen gave me a steady look without saying a word, then turned back to the wheel.

When we arrived in the city centre, she drove up O'Connell Street and on into the north side of the city. This surprised me as she had never driven to this side of town on any of our previous dates.

"Where are you going?"

Helen eyed me. "I thought you said you were leaving it up to me where to go. I just feel like going over here for a change, to see how the other half live."

"Fine."

As we were driving through the unfamiliar streets of north Dublin, it began to rain, just a light drizzle at first but then a more steady flow. The windscreen wiper on my side of the car wasn't working properly; the blade kept getting stuck on the glass. I suggested pulling up so that I could try to fix it, but Helen drove on. "It'll do!"

"Is there something up with you tonight? You're not your usual self."

Helen glanced at me. "What do you mean?"

"I mean you're in a lousy mood!"

Helen gave a false laugh. "Look who's talking about lousy moods! You've been in an almost constant state of gloom and depression for the past five or six weeks, and now here you are preaching to me because I have one off night."

The past few months had been tough for the band: a poorly paid German tour had been followed by a poorly attended English tour; then we had parted company with Billy and Jay and had to break in two replacement musicians.

"It hasn't been an easy time."

Helen pulled a long face. "You're not the only one with problems, you know."

"I didn't say I was. I'm sorry if I took it out on you."

"It doesn't matter."

We came to Ballymun, an estate of high-rise corporation apartments. Helen parked the car in front of one of the huge tower blocks and gazed out at the grim building. "A horrible place, isn't it?"

"What possessed you to come here?"

Helen shrugged. "I just felt like it, that's all."

"It suits your mood."

A young woman wheeling a pram went by the front of the car and made her way towards the graffiti-scrawled entrance to the tower block. Helen sat up and watched her. "Can you imagine what it must be like living in there?"

"Depressing, I'd imagine. But the people who live there are probably used to it."

Helen frowned. "I'd never get used to living in a place like that. I'd crack up, I really would."

"Be thankful you haven't to live there then."

"I am, very thankful."

Helen switched on the engine and started driving back to town.

During the return journey, I suggested going to a bar in the city centre, but Helen wasn't in the mood for drinking. "I have a bit of a headache. I think I'll have an early night, if you don't mind?"

"Fine."

When we arrived at the flat I started getting out of the car, but Helen put her hand on my shoulder. I though it was a gesture of reconciliation, but when I turned and faced her she wasn't smiling. She looked at me for a moment without saying anything, then started rubbing her neck. "There's something I want to tell you." She paused briefly and took a breath. "I've been giving our relationship a lot of thought lately, and I've come to the conclusion that we're not really suited to one another."

I sat in stunned silence.

Helen clutched the steering wheel and looked straight ahead. "I'm sorry, but that's the way I see it."

"What do you mean, not suited?"

"We have nothing in common."

"Nothing?! What have we been doing together for the past five or six months?"

"You've been away a lot of the time."

"No, I haven't. I've been away seven or eight weeks at the most."

Helen kept rubbing her neck. "It's not just that."

"What is it, then?"

"I don't know; it just doesn't seem right any more?"

I looked at the dissolving rain on the windscreen. Everything was blurred. A visit I'd made to Helen's house for tea a few days earlier came into my head. All through the meal, her mother had quizzed me about my plans for the future.

"This wouldn't have anything to do with the grilling your mother gave me the other evening about my future prospects, would it?"

Helen sighed. "I've told you my reasons. You can believe me or not, but as far as I'm concerned it's over between us. Let's leave it at that!"

"If that's the way you want it, fine!"

I got out of the car. Before closing the door, a thought came into my head. I bent down and gave Helen a hard look. "I think I see now why you drove me to Ballymun!"

Helen gave me a puzzled look. "What are you talking about?"

"You're the one who's good at reading into people's characters by the state they keep their houses in. You probably think Ballymun is the kind of place I'll end up in, and you don't want to end up there with me. That's it, isn't it?"

I closed the car door before she had a chance to answer and walked away.

The flat was in darkness when I let myself in. Phil wasn't home. Without switching on the light, I went to the window and looked out. Helen's mini was gone. I felt a sudden sinking sensation in my stomach. I went to the kitchen and took a bottle of whiskey from one of the presses. It was half full. I gulped back most of it without bothering to use a glass. It didn't make me feel any better. A cloying sense of claustrophobia came over me. I felt I had to get out of the flat as fast as I could.

Outside it was still raining, coming down in buckets, but this made no difference to me. I started making my way down Angelsea Road towards Ballsbridge. By the time I got there, my jacket was soaked through to the lining. I went into a bar and had a double whiskey and a pint of Guinness in quick succession. Back on the streets, I started making my way to Blackrock.

Halfway there, I turned off the main road and followed a narrow walkway through some swampland towards the sea. I came to a railway track and tripped going over the sleepers. With my head on one of the iron rails, I started laughing. "Maybe I'll stay here and end it all." I stood up, wobbled down an embankment and came to a granite wall, which I cleared in a single bound. I was on the beach. I sat in the wet sand and started singing one of the songs I'd written for Helen:

> I want to try and say all that I have to say
> For it's the only way you'll know about me
> You need some time to think on things that I say
> I need to know the truth about you and me
> Nothing can go right till I see if you'll be my bride
> My songs are my guide.

I sang the chorus a second time and then sat back in the sand laughing at the old fashioned sound of the word "bride".

"Well, at least I know now that she's not going to be my bride." I picked up a stone and threw it towards the sea.

I remained on the beach for over an hour, staring out into the black ocean, muttering nonsense to myself. Then I hopped up and started making my unsteady way home.

A pathetic looking mongrel dog started following me. I tried to hunt it away, but it kept tagging along at my soggy heels. The mad idea came into my head that I should name the dog. I reversed the letters of Helen and came up with Neleh.

"Here, Neleh. Good dog, Neleh. No home to go to, have you? Nobody wants you either, poor doggy."

The dog was still following me when I entered the flat. I switched on the light. Phil was asleep in bed. The dog started barking. Phil's eyes opened and he noticed the dog. He looked at me and shook his head; then he got out from under his blankets in his underwear and chased the dog around the room. Eventually he caught it by the scruff of the neck and hauled it outside. When he returned to the room, he got back into bed and started scratching his black fuzzy hair. "Are yous bleedin' mad or what, Johnny? That mongrel looked like it had the mange. You're pissed! Get out of those wet things and into bed before you get pneumonia. You look like a drowned rat."

THE RED SCARF

The world keeps turning on us
But we keep getting up with the sun
SONG JOURNAL

THE SOUND OF the front door opening brought me to consciousness. The light was on, but I couldn't open my eyes wide enough to see properly. A taste of blood and alcohol made me gag. I tried to prop myself up in the armchair, but a sharp pain in my right side held me back. I groaned and began to feel other aches and pains in various parts of my body. The door opened and the blurred images of Phil and Gary came into the room. Phil noticed me first. He dropped a canvas bag he was carrying and rushed over to the armchair where I was slouched by the electric fire. "Jasus, what happened to you? Yous're covered in blood."

I tried to focus on Phil's mulatto face. "I got beaten up."

Gary came towards me with one hand over to his mouth. "Who did it to you?"

I opened my lips to speak, and a dart of pain spread from my left jaw. "Ann Marie's boyfriend. You know, the girl whose been calling here to see me lately. He got out of hospital this evening and came here unexpectedly and found us drinking together."

Phil shook his head. "Christ, he really did you in!"

Gary cursed. "Where does the bastard live? We'll go after him and give him a taste of his own medicine."

I shook my head. "No, no. It was my own fault. I shouldn't have been messing around with Ann Marie."

Phil touched my shoulder. "That didn't give him the right to do this to you, the bollix!"

I leaned forward and groaned. "I'll be all right. He took me by surprise; didn't give me a chance to say anything, just lashed into me. I was kinda drunk, so I couldn't defend myself properly. Ann Marie was roaring her head off trying to stop him, but he was like a lunatic."

Gary picked up a red chiffon scarf from the floor. "This must be hers, is it?"

"Yeah."

Phil glanced at the scarf and turned to me. "How come she left you in this state?"

I tried to smile. "You'll never guess? She went off with him in the end."

Gary threw the scarf on a chair. "The bitch!"

Phil laughed. "That's women for you! They lure you along, get your head kicked in and then scarper with the victor. Typical! We'd better try and get you fixed up and put you to bed."

Phil went off and got a basin of hot water from the kitchenette and washed the blood from my face. Then he and Gary helped me out of my bloody clothes and put me to bed. Lying on my pillow, I felt a lot better, though my jaw was still throbbing.

Phil took the basin back to the kitchenette and threw the bloody water down the sink. When he returned to the room, he took off his suit, shirt and tie and placed them neatly on a hanger in the wardrobe. He then got his canvas bag and took it to his bed, glancing at me as he went. "The TV Club was a dead loss tonight. You missed nothing; there was hardly anyone there. I couldn't even pull a decent chick."

I raised myself a little in the bed. "Who was playing?"

Phil shrugged. "Some mickymouse showband. Can't remember their name. Can you, Gar?"

"I never notice bands' names unless I like what they're playing." Gary pulled a light mattress out from under my bed and placed it in front of the

154

fireplace. I watched him throwing blankets over it. "I can't believe you went to the TV Club, Gar!"

Gary shrugged. "The first and the last time! The pricks at the door didn't want to let me in because I wasn't wearing a tie. Did you ever hear the likes? If I told my mates back in Belfast, they'd laugh their heads off. Luckily the manager of the place – Sharky, is that his name? – recognised me from a photo of our band in last week's *Spotlight* magazine."

Phil took a pair of jeans from his canvas bag and placed them neatly across the back of the chair beside his bed. "I warned you you were going to have trouble getting in the way you were dressed. Why do you think I go to all the hassle of taking two sets of clothes to town every Monday night?"

I laughed. "It isn't only Monday nights you do that, Phil."

Phil pouted his lower lip and grinned. "I have me image to protect. Can't go poncin' around the Bailey and Grafton Street in me suit, can I?"

Gary picked up Phil's acoustic guitar from the top of a case lying near the wardrobe and did a few lightening runs down the fretboard. Phil gave him a hard look. "Not at this hour, Gar. The woman upstairs'll be complaining again."

Gary put down the guitar and took off his dirty jeans and crumpled shirt and threw them in a ball on the floor beside his mattress; then he got under the covers without arranging them in any kind of order. "Must be after two, is it?"

I shook my head. "One of us is going to have to get a watch."

Before getting into bed, Phil turned out the light and drew back the curtains, letting in a shaft of amber light from one of the street lamps on Anglesea Road. "I hope you don't mind, Johnny? I don't want to sleep it out in the morning. We have a photo session at half eleven, and I want to make sure the lads in the band are decked out all right before we go to the studio."

I moved down in my bed. "I have to be up early myself. We have a rehearsal organised for eleven. The van'll be picking me up at about a quarter to."

Gary looked at me from his mattress. "How're you going to sing in the state you're in?"

I drew a breath. "I'll get through it all right, but we have a gig tomorrow night I'm worried about. Hopefully the swelling'll be gone down by then.

If it isn't, I'm going to have to wear a mask going on stage, like the phantom of the opera."

Gary cursed in his thickest Belfast accent. "I think we should get that prick and teach him a lesson! You can't let him get away with this."

"I'd prefer to leave it, really. I should never have allowed Ann Marie to call here in the first place. It started innocently enough. On the night the boyfriend went into hospital, she called to see me. Said she was lonely. I took her for a drink, and it moved on from there. I like her, but I swear we never did anything apart from a bit of close kissing. But I knew I was playing with fire. It's my own fault."

Phil laughed. "With my reputation, I'm the one you'd think would end up gettin' beaten up. But I swear, in all my two- and three-timing years, I've never once had an angry boyfriend attack me. Yous're just not lucky in love, Johnny. First your steady drops you, then the boyfriend of that bird from Ballybunion you shifted comes gunning for you, and, oh yeah, what about that recent affair in the pad in Ballsbridge?"

Gary cleared his throat. "What affair was that?"

Phil chuckled. "It happened a week or so before you moved in with us. Tell him, Johnny."

I shifted in the bed. "It's too long a story. Every word I speak makes my jaw ache."

Phil turned on his pillow. "I'll tell him so. A few weeks back, Johnny met up with two kinky birds in the Bailey who invited him back to a classy pad in Ballsbridge for an orgy."

I laughed, causing a sharp spasm of pain in my jaw. "It wasn't like that at all. There was no talk of an orgy to begin with. I fancied one of the girls and thought I might be able to get off with her if I went back with them, that's all."

Phil laughed. "Yeah, but his romantic plan went off the rails when the other bird – an old crow of about forty – didn't like the way Johnny was showing all his attention to the friend. To counteract this development, she broke open a bottle of brandy and suggested a *ménage à trois*."

"A what?!"

"A gang-bang."

Gary started laughing. "I don't believe it!"

"Yeah, tell him, Johnny."

I had my hand over my mouth to stop the pain of laughing. "For Christ sake, Phil, stop will you! My jaw's killing me!"

Gary went on laughing. "What happened, tell us?"

I glanced at the silhouette of Gary's bobbing head. "Nothing happened. I kept trying to shift the good-looking one, and her friend got mad in the end. A row broke out, and I ended up calling the older one a pervert. She asked me to leave after that."

Phil's eyes shone in the amber light. "Would you believe it?! The opportunity of a lifetime and he blew it. He got back here at about four in the morning, pissed as a coot. When he told me what had happened, I was eaten up with jealousy, thinking of how I would have handled the situation."

Gary cleared his throat. "I think I'd have done the same as Johnny. I'm not into that kinky kind of stuff."

Phil whistled. "I believe you, Gar, but thousands wouldn't."

I rubbed my jaw. "We're not all interested in just the one thing, Phil."

Phil laughed. "Tell me that in the morning when you wake up and look at yourself in the mirror. Now I'm goin' to sleep. I have to be out of here before half ten in the morning. Goodnight."

"Goodnight, Phil. Night, Gar."

"Goodnight, lads."

Because of the throb in my jaw, I found it hard to sleep. Lying on my back, I started thinking about Ann Marie. Our first kiss of a few nights before came back to me. We were sitting by the electric fire drinking Martini when I made some innocent remark about the freckles around her nose. She laughed and told me that they were false. Not believing her, I went over and rubbed one of them with my finger. It vanished, and the two of us started laughing. Ann Marie grabbed my finger and got to her feet. She looked into my eyes, and the next think I knew we were in one another's arms. While we were kissing, I remember thinking that what we were doing was wrong, not just because it was a betrayal of Ann Marie's boyfriend, but also because I had no real feelings of love towards her. Despite this, I was enjoying the thrill of feeling her lean body pressed against me, so I manoeuvred her back on to my bed and went on kissing her.

Thinking about the consequences of this kiss, I realised that I would probably never see Ann Marie again. I asked myself how I felt about this, but before deciding on an answer, I fell asleep.

The sound of the tap running in the kitchenette mingled with Gary's heavy snoring woke me early next morning. A beam of sunlight on the wall opposite my bed had replaced the shaft of amber lamplight of the night before. The beating I'd received came back to me. I could still feel aches and pains in various parts of my body. I turned on my side and looked towards the kitchenette. Through the glass partition, I could see Phil standing by the cooker. I moved to get up. A sharp pain in my side made me gasp. I forced myself out of bed and went to the wardrobe mirror to take a look at my face. My left eye was almost completely closed in, and my right eye was swollen and had a small gash at the side of the eyebrow. My jaw was also bruised, and my lower lip was swollen and cut, with a crust of dried blood around the wound.

I got into my clothes and went to the kitchen. Phil was standing by the cooker stirring a pot of baked beans. A pained expression came over his face when he turned to me. "Jasus, you look like you were through ten rounds with Mohammed Ali. But at least it's a sunny morning."

I noticed Ann Marie's red scarf tied around his neck. "What's with the scarf?"

Phil touched the chiffon material. "Looks cool, doesn't it? I'm just borrowing it for the photo session. Is that OK?"

I laughed. "I don't think Ann Marie'll be calling for it somehow. But do you not think it looks a bit over the top?"

Phil pouted his lower lip and grinned. "You know me, man: Oscar the second."

I smiled and sat at the table. "I wonder what time it is?"

Phil looked through the glass partition towards the wall above his bed. "Nearly ten, I'd say."

I glanced through the glass at the angle of sunlight he'd taken his reading from. "I should have time for a bath before the van comes. It might make me feel better."

Phil laughed. "It'll take a lot more than a bath to do that. Would you be up to beans on toast?"

"Just the one slice. I'm not sure if I'll be able to eat with my jaw the way it is."

Phil glanced through the glass. "Should I do some for Gar, I wonder?"

"I wouldn't think so. He's snoring like a pig out there. I don't think he has anything on today."

When the toast was ready, Phil dished up the food and poured out two cups of tea. While we were eating, he kept glancing at me and shaking his fuzzy head. "If I was you, I'd go back to bed and wait till the swelling goes down."

"I can't. We have to get some new songs ready. We're booked into the studio in London on Monday week, remember? We're taking the ferry over on the Saturday night. We need all the rehearsing we can get."

Phil shook his head. "Lucky bastards. I wish my band had an international deal."

I swallowed some toast and rubbed my jaw. "How're things going with the gigs?"

Phil drew a breath. "You know yourself, two or three a week, but the bread we're being paid's the pits. It's hard keeping the boys motivated when they haven't even the price of a pint after we come off stage. We need a good manager, like yous."

I glanced through the glass. "Gary's band seem to be doing well?"

Phil shrugged. "I don't take a lot of interest in them since they fired me." He ate in silence for a few moments, then looked through the glass. "Gar was tellin' me last night that they're thinking of moving to London. I think they have some agency over there interested in them."

I forked some beans carefully into my mouth. "Don't worry, Phil, your time will come."

Phil looked down at the beans on his plate. "I wonder will it?"

In Darkness

I have looked at the dark side of life
As well as day I've studied the night
THE DARK SIDE OF LIFE

THE ROOM WAS in darkness except for a low-hanging light above the round coffee table. We were sitting on cushions on the floor, smoking a joint that our bass player, Jim, had rolled. The beam of light above the table was full of swirling smoke. In the background our album, *Honest Injun* (recorded a few months earlier), was playing at fairly loud volume. The dealer who had sold us the hash we were smoking was sitting awkwardly in a semi-lotus position with his head cocked slightly, listening to the record. When the song started fading, he looked across the table at me and nodded. "I don't know why you didn't want to play it for me, man. That's a fine song."

I hunched my shoulders. "It's not the songs I don't like, it's the production."

Jim handed the joint to the dealer. "Johnny had a number of run-ins with our producer during the recording sessions. He was barred from the control room at one point. We were lucky to get the album finished at all."

The dealer looked at me. "How long has it been out?"

161

"A few months."

Another song started playing behind us, one of the love songs I had written for Helen the year before: *I'm going before the summer comes. The magic of the sun reminds me of when I first met you. . .*

I cringed listening to the thin, unnatural sound of my own voice. "The producer made me sing this one through a megaphone. That's why it sounds so weird. I think he was trying to copy some effect the Beatles used."

The dealer laughed and took a third pull from the joint, then passed it to Peters. "Here, mate, you look like you could use this."

Peters gave the dealer a penetrating look and turned away.

We listened to the record in silence for a few moments; then the dealer cleared his throat. "Any chance of it getting into the charts?"

Jim shook his head. "It got some good reviews, but the record company did nothing to promote it. And just after it came out, we split with our manager, which didn't help. It's selling a little in Ireland, but it's doing nothing over here."

The dealer looked at Peters and grinned. "Maybe it's a slow burner, like the joint there."

Peters gave the dealer a sour look and passed the joint to Robby, the band's drummer. "I think it's dead, Robby, but there might be a hit or two left in it."

Robby sucked at the roach and pulled a long face, "Shit, it nearly burned the mouth off me. Who's got the skins? I'll roll another."

The dealer stuck his hand in his pocket and drew out a cellophane bag and a packet of cigarette papers. "No man, this one's on me. I'll roll you one of my specials, a combination of red Leb and some of that black Moroccan I just sold you. It's a dynamite cocktail. Wait till you try it. It'll blow your heads off."

We had only known the dealer a few weeks. Jim had met him in a bar in Hampstead, close to where we were now living. Since then he had sold us small quantities of hash and LSD on a few occasions.

When the joint was rolled, the dealer placed it between his cupped hands and started sucking on his thumbs. After taking three deep pulls he handed it to Peters. "There you go, man. Get that inside you. It might cheer you up."

Peters stared at the dealer and then turned away. After taking three pulls from the joint, his face grew pale and his hands started to shake. He passed the joint to me and lowered his head.

"Are you all right, Peters? You don't look well." I waited for a reply, but he didn't answer. Instead he gave the dealer a suspicious look. The dealer looked back at him and shook his head.

"What the fuck's up with you? Did you see the look he gave me there?"

Without saying a word, Peters got to his feet and made his way across the room to Jim's bed. He sat on the edge of the mattress for a few moments, then lay back and groaned. The dealer shook his head. "Crikey. He's got it bad, hasn't he?"

I glanced across at Peters, then turned to the dealer. "He hasn't been smoking dope that long. It doesn't always agree with him. He's all right on acid, but hash sometimes puts him on edge. He'll be OK in a minute."

The dealer shook his head. "I sensed it the first time I met him; he's one of them paranoid types."

Peters showed no sign of rejoining us, so I went over to the bed to see how he was doing. He had taken off his glasses. His eyes were open, but his hands were still shaking. I sat beside him on the bed and asked him if he was feeling all right. He leaned forward and clutched my arm. "Please, Johnny, ask that guy to leave, will you? He's evil. I can sense it from him."

"Keep your voice down. He'll hear you."

"I don't care. Please ask him to leave."

"I can't go over and ask him to go, just like that. It wouldn't be right."

Peters raised his voice. "But he's evil I tell you!"

The dealer sprang to his feet and came rushing over to the bed with a distorted look on his face. "What the fuck did you say there, mate?"

I stood up. "Listen, he's not himself. That last joint you rolled was very strong. It's really done his head in. He doesn't know what he's saying. I think we should call it a night, and I'll take him upstairs to our room."

The dealer glared at Peters. "I heard what the prick called me. Who the fuck does he think he is?"

"He didn't mean it, I tell you. He's not himself."

"I don't give a wank. No one calls me that and gets away with it!"

Jim and Robby came over to the bed. Jim smiled at the dealer and offered him the joint. "Here, man, take a last few draws and we'll call it a

163

night. We really appreciate the deal you gave us, but we think it would be best if you left now. As Johnny said, we need to take care of our friend here. He's not well."

The dealer hesitated. "I'll go, if that's what you want. I have another call to make anyway. But you should do something with that guy. He's got a big problem and an even bigger mouth!"

After the dealer left, Robby made Peters a cup of strong coffee, but it didn't improve his condition. He remained sitting at the edge of the bed with a frightened look on his face. Jim and Robby gave up trying to make him feel better and went back to the coffee table and started rolling a joint. I remained on the bed with Peters, hoping his state of mind would improve. It didn't. Twenty minutes went by, and he was still tense and nervous. I stood up to get a drink of water, but he grabbed my arm and held me back.

"Please don't leave me, Johnny. I'm afraid."

"What are you afraid of? The dealer's gone."

"I know, but I still feel strange, as though something awful's going to happen. Would you say a prayer for me, please?"

"A prayer?"

"Yeah, a Hail Mary or an Our Father."

I couldn't help smiling. Peters grew angry. "Don't laugh at me. I'm dead serious. I need you to pray for me. Will you do it? Please!"

I started whispering the Lord's Prayer below my breath: "Our Father who art in heaven, hallowed be thy name, thy kingdom come, thy will be done on earth as it is in heaven. Give us. . ."

Peters interrupted me. "No, no, that's no good. Don't be ashamed. Say it out loud. And ask the lads to say it with you."

I looked across the room at Jim and Robby. They had heard Peter's request but showed no sign of responding to it. Peters began to sob beside me. Robby and Jim stood up and came over to the bed. I started saying another Our Father and the two boys joined in.

After we finished the Our Father, Peters asked for more prayers. I looked at Robby and Jim and started a Hail Mary. We went through a whole decade of the rosary. At the end of the final prayer, Jim stopped abruptly and cleared his throat. "That's enough sodality for one night. Now light up that joint, Robby, and let's put on some sounds."

Peters' state of mind improved. He was still a little shaky, but he was able to stand up and walk around the room.

After we smoked another joint, I began to feel tired, so I decided to go to bed. Peters, who shared a room with me on the second floor, came up with me.

When we opened the door of our small bedsit, I got a nasty smell of sour milk. I looked at Peters. "We forgot to bring back the empties again today. Remind me to do it tomorrow, will you?"

I switched on the light, and Peters followed me into the room. Half the floor space was taken up with the mattress I slept on; the other half was littered with books, magazines and clothes. The base of the bed, where Peters slept, was covered in shirts, jeans and tossed blankets.

Peters undressed and got under the covers without bothering to clean up the mess. I opened the window to let in some fresh air, then turned off the light and bedded down on the mattress.

While I was settling down to sleep, Peters shifted on the base of the bed and the springs started to rattle.

"I don't know what came over me down below. I really flipped, didn't I?"

"Don't worry about it. I guess the situation we're in is beginning to get you down."

After a short silence, Peters cleared his throat. "I've been thinking a lot lately about what we're going to do when our money runs out. We have very little left, you know."

Since the band had returned to live in London, we had been surviving on the advance royalties that Peters and myself received for the publishing rights to the songs on our album, but now even that money was beginning to dwindle.

"We've been in worse scrapes than this before and we survived."

Peters took a deep breath. "Yeah, but that was different. That was with the old band. We were like a family then. I don't know how long Jim and Robby will be willing to put up with the way things are at present. Robby's already complaining that he can't live on the fiver a week we're allowing ourselves."

I turned on my back. "Robby isn't the one I'm worried about. I was around at Mac's place earlier tonight, and he told me that he's thinking of enrolling for a classical guitar course at the Royal School of Music. If he does that, it'll only be a matter of time before he leaves the band, wait and see."

Peters coughed. "I've thought of quitting a few times in the past myself, but I just don't know what I'd do if I left. How about you?"

"I don't want to give up."

Peters took a deep breath. "It's been going through my head lately that things might have been different if we'd kept the old band together."

It was on the tip of my tongue to remind Peters that he had been mainly responsible for all the changes in the band's line-up down the years, but I kept my mouth shut because of his poor mental state. I lay in silence listening to his uneven breathing.

"Johnny?"

"Yeah?"

"Do you believe in God? I mean, really believe in him?"

"I'm not sure any more."

"I do. I found a small chapel up in Hampstead last week and I attended mass there last Sunday. It was really nice. I think I'll go back again next Sunday. Would you like to come?"

I hesitated. "I don't know. I'll think about it."

"Do. It would be really good for you."

I smiled at the irony of this remark.

Peters remained silent for a few moments; then he turned towards the wall and yawned. "Goodnight, Johnny. Don't worry, something's bound to turn up soon. Maybe Deram will find us a new manager. That's all we need to get back on our feet."

"Goodnight, Peters."

A HEAVY LUNCH IN FRANKFURT

Heavy loaded minds tend to travel on their own
HEAVY LOADED MINDS

WE ARRIVED AT the small bungalow on the outskirts of Frankfurt at around one o'clock in the afternoon. Our new
manager, JB, had accepted a lunch invitation the night
before from a German acquaintance of his who had
come to meet him at the Boom Boom Club, where the band were in the
middle of a two-week residency. As our van entered the driveway, a big
brown mongrel dog came bounding down the bumpy tarmac followed by
a blonde-haired boy of five or six years of age. A look of surprise came
over JB's face. "That must be Otto's boy, Carl. I didn't think he'd be quite
so big."

Otto and his partner Erma were at the front door to meet us. After some
awkward introductions (Erma had no English), we followed the couple
into a small, sparsely furnished room. There were no chairs, just an
assortment of large patchwork cushions scattered around a wooden floor.
While Erma went to the kitchen to see to the meal, Otto invited us to sit.
"It will be a little time before the food will be ready. Make yourselves
comfortable."

JB hitched up the knees of his pin-striped suit and awkwardly lowered his bulky behind on to one of the cushions. "Interesting decor, Otto. Very Oriental, though it's quite a challenge on a middle-aged pair of knees like mine."

Otto smiled. "You'd like me to get you a chair maybe?"

JB ran his hand over his bald head. "No, no, dear. Now that I'm down I'm fine, really. Though I may need a helping hand getting up again."

Otto looked across to where I was sitting. "I have to apologise for rushing off last night without meeting you. We had to get home to our childminder. I must say I was surprised to find JB managing a rock band. How did you get connected?"

I sat forward on the cushion. "Our record producer heard that he was thinking of getting into band management, and we happened to be on the lookout for a manager. Our timing was right. We were lucky."

JB raised his eyebrows and smiled. "That remains to be seen. This German outing is the first important engagement I've got for the boys outside of England. Getting into band management was a practical decision for me. Having managed the club for the past decade, I thought I may as well capitalise on my experience and try and steer an up-and-coming band like the boys here to the top. I'm not getting any younger, and club management isn't a pensionable profession. I'm hoping we'll all benefit from the collaboration."

Otto glanced at Peters. "If he manages you half as well as he does the club in London, you will be doing well. I did a photographic assignment there for a magazine a couple of years back, and I saw first hand why it's so famous. By the way, how do you like the Boom Boom Club and Frankfurt?"

Peters sat up. "It's great. But JB has us run off our feet since we got here, visiting war memorials and landmarks. Coming to your house is a welcome break for us."

JB laughed. "After jazz and classical music, history is my keenest passion. I'm fascinated by the whole European struggle since the French Revolution. I'm particularly interested in the Second World War period and the rise of the Third. . ."

Young Carl and the dog came running into the room. The dog went straight over and jumped up on JB's lap, knocking him from the cushion on to the floor. Otto grabbed the dog by the collar and led him and the boy out of the room. When he returned he apologised to JB. "You were saying about the war?"

JB ran his hand over his head. "No, no. The boys are bored to death with my history lessons. They've been very patient with me."

Otto switched on a stereo unit and picked out an album from his collection. "I don't have a great selection of rock music, but you like jazz, JB. You might like this new one by Miles Davis."

A jumble of drum beats, saxophone squeaks and piano discords came out of the speakers. JB frowned. "Oh, no, dear. I like some of his earlier stuff, but this is too avant-garde for me. I like my jazz with swing and a lot more melody. Count Basie or Benny Goodman are more my style."

Otto laughed. "My collection doesn't go back that far, I'm afraid."

While we were listening to the music, Otto went to the mantelpiece and took down a small wooden box, which was sitting beside a soapstone statue of Buddha. "I usually have a joint before dinner. It's good for the appetite. You can join me if you like?"

JB smiled. "I warned the boys before coming to Germany not to attempt to bring any dope through customs, so I'm sure they'll appreciate a reefer. I've never indulged myself."

Otto left the room and returned a few moments later with a bottle and a single glass. "As you don't smoke, JB, you will have a drink of schnapps, yes? It's good stuff."

A look of alarm came over JB's face while Otto was filling the glass. "Not so much. You'll make me drunk."

While JB was sipping his drink, he watched us passing the joint around with a look of amusement on his face. "It has always fascinated me why so many musicians take drugs. Even the big bands did it in the old days. I think it must have something to do with the insecurity of the job."

Otto hunched his shoulders. "All artists like to experience something new, like this music. That's why they experiment with drugs."

JB laughed. "No, no, Otto. I can't accept that this muddled confusion we're listening to is art. There's far too much improvisation and freeplay going on. It never resolves itself. It's chaotic. I'm surprised it should appeal to a German like yourself. One always associates Germany with order and structure."

Otto sneered. "I hate this thing order. Structure is a different kettle of fishes. You find structure in chaos. Things come together and build and then they break up and crumble away. You can't hold on to things. That is death. Life is like this music; big changes, dynamic changes going on all the time."

JB smiled. "Yes, but don't you think that order has to be constantly re-established for peace of mind's sake? There's nothing like sophisticated order. Surely that's what art is all about, putting order to the chaos all around us. And you Germans have done it better than anyone else, especially in the realm of music. I'm thinking of Bach, Haydn, Beethoven, Mozart, and all your other marvellous classical composers."

Otto shrugged. "Very few young peoples in Germany listen to these highbrow peoples you talk of. Rock music and jazz are far more in tune with the primitive rhythms that young people want these days. Am I not right, boys?" He looked at me.

I hesitated. "Most modern jazz leaves me cold, too, I'm afraid. It's too confusing."

Otto stared at me. "But life is confusing, especially modern life in big industrial cities."

"I realise that, but I think music should offer an alternative to the confusion, not just mirror it."

Otto grinned. "But you play rock music! Some of that's even more wild than jazz."

"There's lots of rock music I don't like either."

Peters sat forward. "Johnny's been trying to get us to play more and more acoustic folk music over the past few years."

Jim cleared his throat. "I agree with Otto about the primitive thing. We have to keep some of the rawness as well. That's an essential part of rock'n'roll."

JB laughed and looked at Otto. "The boys are always having musical discussions like this, and they always end in argument. Let's change the subject. Maybe you would show the boys some of your photographs."

Otto hesitated. "I don't do so much photography any more. I paint mostly now. I can use my imagination better with a brush. I will show you some of my recent work, if you like."

Otto left the room and came back a few minutes later with two large canvases, one white with yellow squiggles, the other black with the same squiggles in red. "This one's called *Nachtgedanken* or *Night Ray*, the other is *Tagesgedanken*, or *Day Ray*."

I looked at Peters and lowered my eyes.

Erma came to the door and said something in German. Otto smiled and announced that lunch was ready. We struggled to our feet and made our way to the dining room.

Lentil soup was followed by a hot vegetable curry. For dessert, Erma placed a chocolate cake on the table and started cutting it into thin slices. While she was doing this, she said something to Otto in German; then both of them started giggling. Otto pulled himself together and started handing the cake around. "It's a very rich recipe. I advise you not to eat more than one slice."

JB liked the cake so much he took second helpings. "I can't help it; I have a sweet tooth. That's why I'm so wide around the hips. But at my age, it can be excused."

Carl came into the room and spotted the cake on the table. He stood for a moment looking at his father, then came over and tried to take a slice. Otto hit his wrist with the handle of a knife. Carl started crying and ran to his mother. Without offering any explanation for this rough treatment, Otto began pouring coffee.

After the meal, we returned to the living room and Otto put on a John Coltrane album. While we were listening to the swirling saxophone, I began to feel light-headed. I looked across the room at one of Otto's paintings leaning against the wall. The squiggles appeared to be moving. I rubbed my eyes, but the squiggles were still shifting on the canvas.

On the cushion across from me, JB was staring up at the ceiling. I leaned forward and asked him what he was looking at. He gave a nervous laugh. "I thought the roof was coming down on top of me there for a minute. My head is swimming. It must be that schnapps I had before

dinner. I'm not used to drinking so early in the day. I think I'll go outside and get some fresh air."

Otto and Mac helped JB to his feet and walked outside with him. The rest of us followed behind. In the hallway Jim started laughing. "I don't know about you guys, but I'm flyin' like a kite. If you ask me, that cake had a lot more than chocolate in it. I've never felt this stoned after a single joint before."

On the gravel pathway outside the house, JB was groaning and rubbing his eyes. "I feel dizzy. Everything is floating in front of me. You'd better take me back inside. I need to lie down somewhere. I must be coming down with a fever or something."

Jim grinned. "Fever my arse! You're stoned. We're all stoned. That cake you liked so much was spiked. Wasn't it, Otto?"

Otto looked at JB. "I warned you not to take the second slice, but you wouldn't listen. But don't worry, there was only a small quantity of hash and a little mescaline mixed in with the ingredients. Just go with the flow and you'll be fine."

JB's eyes widened. "My God, I'm drugged! What am I going to do?"

Otto and Mac helped JB back into the house and put him lying in one of the bedrooms. He calmed down for a while but then had another panic attack and started imagining that he was going to have a stroke. Mac suggested calling a doctor, but Otto shook his head. "If the police come, we'll all be arrested."

JB went from crisis to crisis during the next few hours. When we eventually got him back to Frankfurt, he insisted on catching the first plane to London so that he could consult his own GP. As for the rest of us, we had a gig to do that night in the Boom Boom Club.

KILLALA BAY

I'm still not sure what I want
But more and more I know what I don't want
SONG JOURNAL

FEW HOURS after the boys took the LSD, Robby found a ladder in the garden and persuaded the others to climb on to the flat roof of the chalet to look at the stars. Not having taken the drug myself, I tried to stop them from going up, but they wouldn't listen to me. From the gravel patio at the back of the house, I called up to them to be careful, then turned and looked out over Killala Bay. Far out at sea a distant light was pulsing. While I was watching the moving beam – trying to figure out if it was a ship's beacon or a distant lighthouse – Peters came to the edge of the roof and whistled down at me.

"Come on up, Johnny. The Milky Way's like a great big light show up here. It's amazing!"

I laughed. "Them stars are millions of miles away, Peters. Being a few feet higher can't make that much difference. I can see them well enough from down here. Be careful."

Jim joined Peters at the roof edge. "Come on, man. Drop a tab and join us. This is one of the best trips we've ever experienced. You're missing it. It's far out."

"I really don't want to."

Jim hunched his shoulders and turned away.

I went back into the house and sat by the fire reading a book. A few minutes later, I heard the ladder rattling outside as the four boys started to come down from the roof. I could see them descending the steps through the glass-panelled double doors. Three quarters way down the ladder, Ed, the band's new guitar player, jumped on to the gravel, and the others followed his example. Robby, who was last to jump, twisted his ankle when he hit the ground. The other's broke into an immediate fit of laughter, and Robby started laughing with them.

"It's a weird sensation. I know it's pain, but it feels kind of nice." Robby picked himself up from the gravel and hobbled into the house with a strained smile on his face. A few minutes later, he stopped deceiving himself and started moaning. "Christ, it's really hurting me now. Has anyone got an aspirin, anything to stop the pain?"

Peters rushed off to the kitchen and returned a few minutes later wringing his hands. "There's none there. What are we going to do now?"

I started laughing. "For Christ sake, Peters, relax. He's only twisted his ankle. It's not the end of the world."

Jim gave me a sharp look and turned to Robby. "I'll roll a joint for you, man. Maybe that'll help relieve the pain."

After Robby took a few puffs from the joint, he said he felt a little better, but his mood didn't improve. He sat nursing his foot with a twisted expression on his face. His condition began to affect the others. They finished smoking the joint without talking and then sat around in glum silence staring at the walls. Eventually the atmosphere became so oppressive I slipped away to the small room I was sharing with Robby and Ed and had an early night.

I woke around eight the next morning. Robby was snoring in the bunk overhead of me, and Ed was breathing heavily in a single bed beside the window. I rose and dressed and made my way to the living room. The place was a shambles, with empty beer bottles, overflowing ashtrays, old newspapers and magazines strewn all over the floor.

I manoeuvred my way through the band's musical equipment, which was set up in various parts of the room, and went out through the glass doors. Outside it was a dull, overcast morning. I took a deep breath of the salty air and looked out over Killala Bay. A single fishing trawler coming from the town of Killala a few miles back the coast was heading out to sea. Watching it, I found myself wishing I was on board the boat, sailing off in a definite course. For a long time now, I had been feeling all adrift in my life. I wasn't exactly sure why. Over the past few months, things had steadily been improving for the band. A successful residency in the Marquee Club in London had been followed by an offer to record a second album with Deram Records. In preparation for these recordings, we had come to Killala to put new songs together, but in the two weeks we'd been here, little had been achieved.

I went back into the house and got my tweed jacket; then I headed down to the beach, taking a narrow tussocky path through the sloping fields. When I reached the strand, I went right to the edge of the foaming water and skimmed a few flat stones over the surging tide. An incoming wave took me by surprise and splashed over my desert boots. I moved back in the sand and set off strolling along the beach.

After walking for a few minutes, I started humming to myself, trying to come up with a melody for a song. I had a good lyrical idea that I'd been mulling over for the past few mornings about a girl I'd met at a gig in Dublin just before coming to Killala. The memory was full of sunlight, bells and Sunday morning kisses, but I hadn't been able to bring it alive in song during the previous days, and my attempt to do it now failed also.

I returned to the chalet and had breakfast, then decided to do some practicing on my new acoustic guitar.

While I was tuning the strings, Peters came into the house through the glass doors. His head jerked when he spotted me. "You gave me a fright there, Johnny. I should have realised you'd be up. I've just been to mass in the little chapel down in the village. I haven't been to bed yet, but I still feel as fresh as a daisy. It's amazing."

I put the guitar down. "Did you not find the service strange on acid?"

"No, it was beautiful. The gospel reading was the miracle of the loaves and fishes, a very trippy story."

"Trippy?!"

"Yeah, the way Jesus magically produced all that bread from nowhere."

"If you can believe it!"

Peters squinted. "Oh, I believe it all right. I really believe it."

"And you can square taking drugs with your faith?"

"Why not? Acid is a mystical drug, almost as mystical as the bread and wine in the Eucharist."

I smiled. "I'm sure the priest who served it to you wouldn't agree with you there. And I don't think there was anything very mystical about what went on here last night. When I left you, you were all totally paranoid. And all because Robby sprained his ankle!"

Peters sat on an armchair opposite me. "That was just a reaction to the accident. Those vibes only lasted an hour or so. After that we had an amazing time. We went for a mind-blowing walk out along the coast road. You should have seen the moon and the silhouettes of the trees; it was magical, really magical. The whole place was vibrating with life. We came upon a horse in a field, and you could feel the air throbbing with energy around it. And the sea was beyond description at dawn. We couldn't see the sun, but the clouds were all pearly and pink, like the inside of a seashell. I swear, the whole trip was one of the best I've ever been on. We're thinking of dropping another tab tomorrow or the day after. Maybe you'll join us?"

I shook my head firmly. "I didn't come here for that. I don't know if you're aware of it, but we've been here now for almost two weeks and we've only managed to arrange one full song. We've only got another week before we return to London, and things are getting worse not better. We came here to work, but everyone seems to be treating it as a holiday. I'm fed up sitting around every morning while the rest of you sleep your heads off. It wouldn't be so bad if we got some work done at night, but we've spent more nights in the pub than we've spent rehearsing. It's madness!"

Peters removed his glasses and wiped the lenses with the tail of his purple caftan. "You're all tensed up, Johnny. I can really feel your anger. But you yourself are partly to blame for the way things have been going. Every arrangement we come up with for your new songs, you criticise. You've lost all interest in rock music, and you expect us to go along with the acoustic direction you're taking. There has to be compromise in a band, but you're unwilling to give an inch."

"Is it wrong of me to have strong opinions about the way my songs should be arranged?"

"No, but we have to have an input, too."

"But some of the boys' ideas are totally whackey. Our biggest problem is that we're stoned all the time. It's impossible to get anything done on hash; it just makes you tired and dopey. And whenever we drop acid, it takes days to level out. That's why I didn't take any yesterday. I really think we should go off all drugs for the remaining time we've got here. That way we might still get something done."

Peters shook his head. "The boys will never agree to that. Jim especially. He couldn't do without his draw. Anyway, I think you're wrong about the cause of our problems. They go a lot deeper than that."

"What do you mean?"

Peters hesitated. "I've had a long night, Johnny. Can we leave this discussion till later?"

"Just tell me what you're getting at, and I'll leave it then."

Peters got to his feet. "As I see it, the main problem we have is that you hardly communicate with the rest of the band any more. You're constantly reading books or practising your guitar. You don't even listen to the same records as we do. You go to bed early and get up sometimes at the crack of dawn. It's irritating for the rest of us. It's as though you're going out of your way to be different."

I shook my head firmly. "That's crap and you know it. I've always been an early riser. And as for listening to different records, I see nothing wrong with that. Just because I'm part of a band doesn't mean I have to share the same taste in music as the rest of you. I've always followed my own heart when it comes to songs."

Peters sighed. "It's not just the music, Johnny. You're whole attitude to rock'n'roll has changed. You're even beginning to dress different than the rest of us."

I looked out through the glass doors and noticed a slight break in the clouds above the bay.

"What's so wrong with being different?"

ALONE

The moon was hidden in dark clouds
And I was alone
GOING MY OWN WAY

THERE WAS A heavy knock at the door. I looked up from the book I was reading on my mattress on the floor.

"Come in, it's open."

Robby put his head round the edge of the door and smiled down at me. "What are you up to?"

"What does it look like, Robby?"

Robby stepped into the room and sat on the base of the bed. "What's the book?"

I showed Robby the cover of the paperback in my hand. He laughed. "*The Devils*! Christ, I though Peters was bad reading the Bible all the time, but this takes the biscuit."

"It's a book about Russian revolutionaries, Robby."

"Oh." Robby put his hand through his hair and cleared his throat. "Listen, why don't you come downstairs and join us. All the boys are there. You don't have to smoke dope, if you don't want to. Just come down and be with us. We've been discussing the album."

I grinned. "We've been doing that since we got back from Ireland over a month ago. It's not talking we should be doing but practising new songs."

"Well, why not come down and say your piece."

"I've said it already, a dozen times."

"Say it again."

I hesitated. "It's late, Robby. I was just going to go to bed."

Robby stood up. "Please come down, just for a while. Peters asked me to ask you."

I took a deep breath and got to my feet. "OK, but I don't intend staying long. I hate this sitting around yammering all night, especially when you're all stoned. It gets us nowhere."

Downstairs I followed Robby into his and Jim's dimly lit bedsit. I winced at the smell of marijuana. Jim, Peters and Ed were slouched in various parts of the narrow room with sleepy expressions on their faces, passing around a joint. Joe Cocker's *Mad Dogs and Englishmen* album was playing on the stereo.

Jim was the first to notice my arrival. "Hey, look what the wind's blown in! The long-lost prodigal son's come back to us. Good to see you, man. Sit down and have a blow."

"No, thanks."

Jim persisted. "It's only a bit of draw, man. It'll mellow you out."

"That's what I'm afraid of."

Robby gave Jim a hard look. "If he doesn't want to smoke, don't hassle him. Sit down and make yourself comfortable, Johnny. Would you like a cup of coffee?"

"No, thanks, Robby, I'm fine."

I sat on the edge of Robby's bed and smiled across the room at Peters and Ed. "Robby was saying you were discussing the album?"

Peters took the joint from his mouth. "Yeah, we were just talking about the songs, and we thought you might like to hear what was being said."

"What were you saying?"

Peters leaned forward to answer, but Jim interrupted him by singing along with the song on the stereo.

I smiled at Jim's low-key voice. Jim noticed me smiling. He stopped singing and looked straight at me. "If only we had a few songs like that, man, we'd really be in business."

I listened to the song for a moment. "You think that's a good song, do you?"

"Yeah, man, I do. It's got a great groove. Listen to the band; they're really cookin'."

I listened. "The band may be cookin', but the song's a bit hard-boiled, don't you think?"

Jim looked at me. "What do you mean?"

"I mean, it's not a great song, is it?"

Jim sneered. "And you think your songs are?"

"I didn't say that."

"No, but that's what you meant."

"It isn't what I meant. I don't think my songs are great. They're just the best I've managed to come up with. And none of you have come up with anything better."

Jim looked down at his cowboy boots. "We've just been comparing your new songs with the songs you wrote for the first album, and we don't think they're half as good."

"Who's *we*?" I looked round the room at the others. Robby and Ed avoided my gaze. Peters turned towards me but avoided my eyes. "All Jim's saying is that the standard of your new numbers isn't as high as before, that's all."

"How do you know? You've only tried arranging two of them. I have six others."

Peters took the glasses from his nose and started rubbing his eyes. "Yeah, but you've played them to us a few times. The words are OK, but there's no groove in the rhythm."

"I didn't write them with a groove in mind."

Jim grinned. "That's the problem, man. You're in a different space than the rest of us."

"Different space?"

"Yeah, you're turning straight, man. Dead straight!"

"What's wrong with being straight?"

Jim grinned. "It ain't rock'n'roll."

I took a deep breath. "Listen, I'm really sick to my teeth of that old cliché. If your idea of rock'n'roll is sitting around getting stoned out of your heads like a bunch of zombies seven days a week, then you're right,

I don't want anything to do with it."

Jim glared at me. "Did anyone ever tell you you're a bollix, man? A prize bollix!"

"No. But it's good to know how you feel about me, Jim. I'll keep it in mind."

Jim sneered. "Man, you don't know the fucking half of it! I despise you! You're the last fucking person in the world I'd want to live with."

I laughed. "We're lucky we're not sharing the same room then, aren't we?"

Jim grinned. "Yeah, from what I hear from Peters, I'm very lucky."

I turned to Peters. "What exactly did he hear about me from you, Peters?"

Peters squirmed in his chair. "Nothing. I just said you don't talk very much these days. Which you don't. You're always reading books. I don't know when was the last time you even said good morning to me."

I laughed. "Maybe that's because you never get up until the afternoon, and I'm usually in Hampstead Heath by then, trying to write songs."

"You know what I mean, Johnny."

"No, I don't. I haven't a clue what's going on here, except that it's obvious you've been talking about me behind my back."

Robby started to leave the room. "I hate these arguments. I'm going to the shop for milk."

Ed stood up and followed Robby. "Hold on and I'll be with you. I need to get some fags."

After the two boys left the room, I got to my feet and started walking towards the door. Peters called me back. "Hang on a minute, Johnny. There's no point in taking offence like this. We need to discuss this matter."

"Discuss?!"

"Yeah. You're reading too much into what Jim said. You provoked him by calling us zombies."

"He provoked me first."

"Yeah, well, we still need to thrash out the problem of the songs for the album. JB phoned again today telling us that Deram are becoming impatient waiting to find out when we're going to start recording. We need to come to a decision soon."

I took a deep breath. "You've told me you don't think my songs have enough groove, so I guess we're at stalemate."

Jim grinned. "Wrong, man. You're at stalemate. We know we don't want to record those songs of yours. We're sure of that. So maybe there's only one thing left to do."

"What's that, Jim?"

Jim looked down at his cowboy boots. "Go our separate ways, I guess."

"Break up?"

Jim hesitated. "Not exactly. We can go on with Robby as our singer. He's been getting a great reaction on stage to that Leon Russell song that you refused to sing."

I looked at Peters. "Is this what you want, too?"

Peters hesitated. "It isn't what I want. But I can't understand your reluctance to sing other people's songs. We started out doing cover versions. Look at Joe Cocker there, he does nothing but covers and see how successful he is."

I felt a catch in my throat. "I don't want to do covers. I want to find my own voice."

Peters looked at me. "I don't know what you mean, Johnny. You already have a very distinctive voice."

"I don't just mean my singing voice; I mean the things I sing about."

Peters looked away. "Your new songs don't suit the band. We've tried them, Johnny, and they just don't work for us."

I cleared my throat. "Well, what are we going to do then?"

Peters looked down at the floor. "Maybe you'd be happier going your own way. I can see no alternative to that, unless you have some other idea?"

I walked over and stood in front of Peters. "What's the point in asking me a question like that? You've obviously made up your mind that you want me out of the band. Good luck to you!"

I left the room and went upstairs, trembling with anger. I was too upset to think of going to bed, so I got my jacket and headed out for a walk.

Though it was after midnight, I made my way to Hampstead Heath. After walking for ten or fifteen minutes on one of the main pathways, I branched on to a dirt track that led to a pond I was in the habit of going to on my songwriting treks each morning. When I got there, I sat on a bench overlooking the dark pond. The place was a mass of pitch-black shadows. A cold breeze shook the leaves of the branches overhead. I began to shiver. Peters and Jim came into my mind. I thought of their criticism of my new songs and admitted to myself that they were probably right. I cursed and began to cry. For three or four minutes, I poured my eyes out; then I got up and started walking. I went right into the heart of the heath, to an area I'd never been to before. I came to an iron bridge overgrown with ivy and other foliage. I looked over the iron rail. There was no water down below, just dense weed and dark bracken. I drew a deep breath and moved back to the centre of the bridge. I looked up into the night sky. There was nothing visible up there; no moon or stars, not a pick of light. The black leaves of the bushes and trees around me began to rattle in the breeze. I turned back but couldn't find my bearings. Darkness faced me everywhere I looked.

BACK HOME

I remember as a boy sitting by the fire pondering on a dark night
And my mother's warm voice saying to me, "You're a dreamer!"
WHAT GOD ONLY KNOWS

GLANCED AROUND the grey ward to see if any of the patients were looking at me, then took a small nickel medal of St Christopher from my
jacket pocket and handed it to my mother. "I got it from a monk I met
in Frankfurt one day when I was out walking. I was taking a rest on a
bench just outside the city, and he came along and started talking to me.
He said it would bring me peace and maybe a bit of luck. I'd like you to
have it. It may bring you some."

My mother smiled mischieviously. "It didn't bring you a lot, did it?"

"I don't know about that. Just because the band's gone doesn't mean
that I've given up. Going solo might turn out to be the best thing that ever
happened to me."

My mother looked me straight in the eyes. "You were always a dreamer.
Even when you were a small boy. You got that from your father."

I laughed. "I think I remember Dad saying that it was from you I got that
particular trait."

"Oh, no. Your father was much more of a dreamer that I ever was. Did
you know he wrote poetry when he was young?"

I widened my eyes. "Really? I always thought of Dad as a very practical, down-to-earth sort of man. I can't imagine him ever having had flights of fancy."

"How do you think he became attached to a feather-brain like me? He was very romantic in his younger years. Having to cope with me knocked a lot of the stuffing out of him, but he still has his moments."

A patient sitting beneath a picture of Our Lady at the opposite side of the ward gave a loud grunt and then sat back in her chair, drooling at the mouth. I watched her for a moment, shuddering inside, then turned back to my mother. "I called to see Joan in Birmingham before I left England a month ago. She seems happy enough in her marriage."

My mother sat up. "She writes regularly. Kay and Pattie are happy in their marriages, too. They were up to see me last night. They're good girls. The boys are good, too."

I smiled. "What do you think of the drawing Michael did on our bedroom ceiling. It's like the Sistine Chapel. He's quite an artist, isn't he?"

My mother raised her head. "He has his heart set on art college. And Eric loves it in the NIHE. Barry and Sue miss me when I'm up here, but I should be going home soon."

I sat forward. "I hardly know Barry or Sue. They were tiny when I left home. It's hard to believe that that was only five years ago."

My mother smiled. "Time flies when you're having a good time."

I raised my eyebrows. "I wouldn't exactly say that the last five years have been a good time for me."

My mother started getting to her feet. "What do you mean? You've done more in them five years than most people do in a lifetime. Count yourself lucky. Up here time drags by so slowly it often feels like we're not even alive. Who ever though of the term 'patient' knew exactly what they were thinking of. You need infinite patience in a place like this. Wait here for a moment; I have to get a cigarette."

My mother looked thin and frail making her way across the room to the glass-panelled office. She had aged a lot since I'd last seen her. I watched her through the glass, joking with the nurse, which wasn't characteristic of her. When she returned to where I was sitting, she had a cigarette burning in her mouth. "They don't allow us keep our own because the patients keep bumming them from us. It's an awful nuisance, but I should be going home soon. I'm feeling a lot better. They've changed my tablets, and Dr

Toomey says I'm a lot more stable now. By the way, what do you think of my hair? I had it done this morning. Nurse Brennan was just complimenting me on it."

While I was praising my mother's perm, a woman in a soiled cardigan approached us and asked for a cigarette. My mother touched the woman's trembling hand and smiled. "You know yourself, Mary, they only give them out one at a time. I'll get you one later on, OK, love?"

Mary muttered something under her breath and retreated to a chair in a far corner of the ward. My mother shook her head. "Poor Mary. She came in last week. Been here before. She tried to burn her house down last Christmas. Her poor husband's gone up the walls with her. He visits her every evening, but she doesn't pay him much heed. By the way, I've been meaning to ask you, how've you been getting on with your father since you came home?"

I sat forward. "He took me out for a pint last night. I showed him a cheque for a thousand pounds that I got from the band when we parted company – royalty money I was owed for my songs, plus my share of the van and musical equipment. That impressed him. He gave me some advice on how to invest it. We're getting on fine. But he's worried about you."

A stem of ash fell from my mother's cigarette. "He's been very patient with me down the years. It hasn't been easy for him. He hates coming up here, but he comes regularly nonetheless. But I should be well enough to go home soon. How long are you stopping yourself?"

"Just a few days. I have to get back to Dublin and find myself a flat. I have a few friends in the music business there who've promised to help get me work on the folk circuit. I'll be fine."

My mother took my hand. "I hope so. I'll be praying to the Holy Spirit for you. And don't be worrying about me whatever you do. I'm almost back to normal as it is. I'll be seeing Dr Toomey again tomorrow for our game of cat and mouse."

"Your what?"

"It's just the name I have for our therapy sessions."

I smiled. "You're the mouse?"

"No, no; I'm the cat. Dr Toomey's the mouse. I run rings round him. But he's a lovely man. I'm hoping he'll give me the all-clear tomorrow. Then I'll be able to go home at the weekend."

A few patients started setting dining tables in a far corner of the room. Among them I recognised a few faces I'd seen during previous visits to the hospital. Most of them were chatting and joking.

"They look happy enough."

My mother took a pull from her cigarette. "Lunchtime is the highlight of our day up here. But here, it's time you were going. You've been here long enough." She stood up. "I'll call Nurse Brennan, and she'll let you out. I really enjoyed the visit. I hope you'll call again before you go back to Dublin."

"I'll come tomorrow at the same time, around eleven."

The nurse unlocked the ward door with a large key. I kissed my mother and started to leave. As the door was closing behind me, I turned back and noticed a look of deep sadness in my mother's eyes. I shivered and walked on.

Outside the hospital I started to cry. A car came up the driveway towards me. I wiped my eyes with the back of my hand and walked on towards the gate.

On Mulgrave Street, I cut down by Limerick Jail and made my way home through Prospect and People's Park. When I arrived at our house, I found my father in the kitchen having his lunch with the racing page of a daily newspaper lying beside his plate. He looked at me over the rims of his reading glasses. "There's some stew there that Nancy made. Fill yourself a plate. None of the others come home for lunch when your mother's in hospital. They go to Nancy's instead."

"No, thanks, Dad, I'm not hungry. I'll have it later."

"Please yourself. How did you find your mother?"

"A little high, maybe, but in full control of herself. We had a nice chat. I'll go up again tomorrow."

My father frowned. "You should have been here last week when she was getting up at three and four in the morning, disrupting the whole house."

I sat opposite my father. "She's seeing Dr Toomey tomorrow. She thinks he might give her the all-clear for coming home at the weekend."

My father shook his head firmly. "She's better off staying up there for a while."

"But it's such a dismal place, Dad. And she didn't seem that bad to me."

My father stopped eating. "She upsets the whole house when she's the way she is. I can't cope with her any more. She's getting worse all the time. She threw her arms around a bus conductor two weeks ago and tried to dance with him on a moving bus."

I laughed. "Has she not been taking her tablets, or what?"

"She keeps the capsules under her tongue sometimes and spits them out when we're not looking. It's not her fault, but she has my heart broken." My father lowered his head and started to cry. This was the first time he'd ever done this in front of me. I got up from my chair and went over and put my hand on his shoulder. I didn't say anything; I just stood there for a few moments till he stopped crying, then I went back and sat on my chair.

My father finished his lunch in silence, then stood up from the table. "I'd better hurry or I'll be late. You're staying for another few days, aren't you?"

"Till the day after tomorrow."

"I'll see you later then. Maybe we'll go out for a pint again tonight?"

"I'd like that."

When my father reached the kitchen door, he looked back at me. "Don't worry about your mother; she'll be fine in a few weeks. It never lasts longer than that. But she's better off up there until then, for her own good."

After my father left the house, I went upstairs and lay on my old single bed. The ceiling above me was covered with a huge pencil drawing of Michelangelo's *Creation of Adam*. The shading on Adam's outstretched arm brought out all its muscular strength. As I studied it, I calculated that my brother Michael was fourteen.

In a cubbyhole beside the bunk beds I noticed a cassette of Bach's *Brandenburg Concertos*, owned by my brother Eric, and some Superman comics belonging to my brother Barry. I leaned over and took a copy of *Don Quixote* from the windowsill, where I'd left it earlier that morning.

After reading a few pages, I began to feel tired. I put my head back on the pillow and nodded off. Some time later, I was woken by the sound of the front door opening downstairs. I hopped up and went down to see who had come into the house.

In the kitchen, my sister Kay was filling the kettle. Her head jerked when she spotted me. "When did you get home?"

"Yesterday afternoon."

She looked me up and down and smiled. "It's great to see you. We were expecting you weeks ago after we heard about you splitting from the band."

"I had things to do in Dublin. I'm going to base myself there."

She plugged in the kettle. "You won't be coming back to live in Limerick so?"

I sat at the table. "Dublin's where the action is."

Kay rinsed out the teapot. "What are you going to do there?"

"Write songs and sing. What else?"

"Without a band?"

"Yeah, solo." I sat back in the chair. "How are Sue and Martin?"

Kay shook her head. "Sue's great. She'll be starting school next year. You'll have to come out to the house and see her before you go back."

"I'll go out tomorrow afternoon."

The kettle started to boil. Kay made a pot of tea and put it on a cooker ring to draw.

"I was up to see Mam. She's in good form."

A strained look came over Kay's face. She placed two cups on the table, one in front of me. "I come in a few times a week to make sure Dad has enough groceries when she's in hospital."

"She's hoping to get home by the weekend."

Kay's face stiffened. "I hope you didn't tell her she'd be coming out?"

"No, but she seemed quite well."

Kay gave a false laugh. "She'd fool a saint, that woman."

I looked down at the empty cup. "But it's such an awful place up there."

Kay came towards me with the teapot. "Who are you telling? Pattie and myself have been visiting her two and three times a week every time she's been in there over the past five years. How many times have you been up there during that time?"

I took a deep breath. "I always made it a point to go and see her whenever the band were in Ireland. You know that."

Kay started pouring tea into my cup. "Sorry for snapping. It's just that the last couple of years have been quite a strain. Pattie and myself have been left here to pick up the pieces. Joan writes home from England every now and again giving instructions about what should be done. It can be very frustrating. On top of that, things aren't going well between Martin and myself."

"Sorry to hear that." I tried to think of something consoling to say, but nothing came. "Now that I'll be living in Dublin, I'll try and get home more often."

Kay sat opposite me. "It isn't going to be easy for you without a band. What are you going to live on?"

"I have a bit of money that'll keep me going, and I'm hoping to get gigs in folk clubs around the country. I'll get a job, too, if I have to. I'll be fine. My aim is to get a solo record deal back in London. I've already sent off some demos of new songs. I haven't heard anything back yet, but I'm hopeful."

Kay gave me a doubtful look and lowered her eyes.

OVERLAPPING

Out on my own with no place to call home
MOLLY

I WAS PUTTING paste on the first sheet of wallpaper when the phone started ringing in the downstairs part of the house. Mrs Brunn called from the bottom of the stairs.

Victor, a fellow musician who was helping me with the job, went down to see what she wanted and came back a few moments later with a worried look on his face. "She needs to know what kind of paint her husband should get for the ceilings. He's in a paint shop in town right now waiting for an answer. What will I tell him?"

I scratched my head. "Is it emulsion?"

Victor gave me a blank look. "What are you asking me for, hey? You're the one who claimed to know all about painting and decorating when you put the ad in the paper for the job. I'm only your helper, remember?"

I shook my head, irritated by Victor's Northern Ireland drawl. "I never claimed to know all about it. I just said I'd helped my father out a few times wallpapering and painting our house when I was growing up."

Victor cursed. "Well, what am I going to tell him? He's waiting on the phone for an answer."

I took a deep breath. "Just tell him to get good quality ceiling paint."

Victor looked at me doubtfully. "Good quality?"

"Yeah, the best quality the shop has."

Victor went downstairs and came back a few minutes later with his hand over his mouth, trying to stop himself from laughing. "I told him but he sounded a bit suspicious. He kept saying Good Quality, as though it was a brand name. I don't think he's on to us, though. His wife spoke to him after he talked to me, and before I came upstairs, she told me that any time we want coffee to let her know and she'll make it for us. She's a nice woman, hey. I hope we don't mess up her house."

"We won't, don't worry. Now help me get this wallpaper up before the paste dries. The first sheet is always the trickiest. That's why I hung that string from the ceiling, to get a straight line that we can work from."

While we were putting up the second sheet, I noticed that there was no border area for overlapping the paper. This puzzled me because, as I remembered it, my father had always overlapped the wallpaper he had put up in our house. To overcome this problem, I improvised an overlap of a quarter of an inch and made sure that it was evenly spaced from top to bottom.

When we had seven or eight sheets up, Victor looked at his watch. "It's pushin' on, hey. We'd better get down to the Labour and or it'll be closed."

I put down the paste brush. "I'll tell Mrs Brunn we have to leave for a while to inspect another job."

When we arrived at the Labour Exchange, we took our places in separate queues before the hatches. Since I'd started signing on for assistance a month before, I had always managed to get to the office soon after it opened in the morning. At that time the place was usually empty, but now, with just twenty minutes left to go before the hatches closed, the office was packed to capacity.

My turn arrived to approach the teller. Stony-faced, she handed me my card. I picked up the blunted stub of a pencil attached to a dirty piece of chord and signed my initials as best I could, then left the office. Victor was waiting for me outside the building.

On the way back to the job, we bought a couple of sandwiches in a delicatessen. When we arrived at the house, Mrs Brunn made coffee and told us that the paint had arrived. Upstairs we found a large can of emulsion with some smaller tins of gloss paint and varnish.

"You were right, hey; ceiling paint is emulsion."

While we were having lunch, Victor brought up the subject of a gig I was booked to play later that evening. "What time do you go on stage?"

I swallowed some sandwich. "The show begins at half eight, but my spot's not till after ten. I'm really nervous about it."

Victor grinned. "What's to be nervous about? You've played on your own before, haven't you?"

"In noisy bars and clubs. This is different; it's a sit-down concert. People will really be listening."

Victor laughed. "You'll be fine. I wish I could go and see you, but I can't get out of the pub gig I have. I need the money for the insurance for my van anyway."

I bit into my sandwich. "I'm going to use the money I'm getting tonight to record some new songs."

Victor sipped his coffee. "What happened to the last demos you made? You sent them to some companies in England, didn't you?"

I rubbed my eye. "They turned me down. This time I'm going to go to London myself and do the rounds of the A&R offices. That's the only way to do it."

Victor hunched his shoulders. "I wouldn't have the nerve to do that. Good luck with it, hey."

I swallowed my last piece of sandwich and drained my cup. "Come on, we'd better get back to work. I'll finish the papering. You can start painting the ceiling of the other bedroom with a roller. I'll show you how to use it."

After giving Victor some basic instructions on how to use a paint roller, I left him to it and went back to wallpapering. Twenty minutes later, he came to me with white paint splattered all over his auburn hair and freckled face. "I can't seem to get the knack of it, hey. The paint keeps falling off the roller."

I went next door. There was twice as much paint on the protection sheeting on the floor than there was on the ceiling. I cursed. "I think you'd better leave the ceilings to me. You can varnish the wooden banisters on the stairs. Just remember to put the varnish on sparingly or you'll be left with long dripping marks. I'll show you what to do."

A quarter of an hour after I left Victor on the stairs, I went back to see how he was getting on. Amazingly, he had only two rungs of the banister varnished, and both of them were dripping like candles. I grabbed the brush from him and cursed. "You're useless! I'm almost finished papering the first bedroom. You go in any tidy up the loose ends and I'll finish the first coat here."

Despite Victor's incompetence, we managed to get quite a lot of work done during the afternoon. Just as we were knocking off at five-thirty, Mr Brunn arrived home. On his way upstairs, he inspected the banisters and gave me a smile of approval when he reached the landing. We moved into the first bedroom. While he was surveying the walls, a puzzled look came over his face. "Correct me if I'm wrong, but I was under the impression that this kind of vinyl wallpaper should be joined and not overlapped like this?"

I raised my chin. "A lot of people would agree with you, Mr Brunn, but I myself have always been of the opinion that overlapping is essential for durability. This way you won't have any ugly hanging corners after a few months. The slight overlap insures fixability."

Mr Brunn nodded. "Of course, of course. You're the experts. I'll leave it in your capable hands. Do you think you'll have the job completed by Thursday, as you estimated?"

I glanced at Victor's paint-speckled face. "Let's say Friday, to be on the safe side."

After we left the house, we drove to Victor's bedsit in Blackrock. I had left my guitar and some clothes there earlier, knowing there wouldn't be time to return to my flat in Dalkey to change. We cleaned up and had a bite to eat, then drove to town and had a drink in McDaid's bar before parting company.

I arrived at the theatre where I was due to play just before eight. After I did a quick sound check, the promoter showed me to my dressing room. There was a half crate of Guinness sitting on the dressing table, compliments of the main sponsor of the event. I drank three bottles while running over some songs. The show started. While the first few acts were playing my nerves started tingling, so I drank a few more bottles for Dutch courage. By the time I was called to the stage, I was fuzzy headed but full of confidence.

The MC gave me a big build-up by announcing my past credentials, which drew a loud round of applause from the audience. I stumbled out to the microphone and launched into my opening number. In the middle of the first verse, I noticed that my top E string was flat. I waited for an opportune moment and tried to get it in tune but ended up adjusting the wrong tuning head. The song collapsed. A few people at the back of hall started heckling. I apologised and tuned the string. I started another number. The guitar still sounded slightly sour, but I kept going. At the end of the song, the heckling started again. I tried to improve the tuning. My G string snapped. The entire audience broke into a fit of laughing. I groped for my spare strings. Just as I found them, a stage hand rushed towards me with another guitar. "There's no time for changing strings. Use this. It belongs to one of the other singers."

I performed two more songs, then thanked the crowd for their patience and left the stage to a small round of applause. In the wings, the promoter slapped me on the back. "Don't worry, Johnny, everyone has an off night. You did fine under the circumstances."

After I collected my fee, I hurried off to the nearest bar to drown my sorrows. While I was gulping back a beer at the counter, a girl wearing glasses approached me. "Hi, I'm Carmel Snow, a friend of Joan Higgins, remember? I was with her at that gig in UCD a few months back when you were still with your band."

"Oh, yeah. How's Joan keeping? I haven't seen her since I got back to Ireland. I've been meaning to call her."

Carmel smiled. "You've just missed her. She was here all night with Mary, her flatmate. They've just gone home."

I looked at the clock inside the counter. "I'm going to have to leave myself soon to catch the last bus to Dalkey. I live there now."

Carmel smiled. "That's a long way out. Why don't you call up and see Joan. You've stayed in her place before. I'm sure she'd put you up again. I'll phone her, if you like? She should be home by now."

Without waiting for my answer, Carmel rushed off to a phone in the hall and came back a few of minutes later grinning. "You're fixed up. She said she'll wait up for you with a cup of tea."

I shook my head and laughed. "You must like fixing people up, do you?"

197

Carmel grinned. "Wouldn't you know I'm from Clare, the matchmaking county? I have to go now. I'm with a fella over there. He'll think I'm trying to get off with you. Ask Joan for some of her mother's porter cake. It's lovely."

I arrived at Joan's flat just after midnight. I was glad when she, and not her flatmate, opened the door. She looked even better than I remembered.

"I hope I'm not too late?"

"No, no. Mary's gone to bed. I was just listening to the radio. Come in."

A portable radio was playing in the living room. I put my guitar in a corner and sat on a divan in front of an electric fire. I was a little tipsy, but I held myself together and started apologising again for my late arrival. "I was only talking to your friend for a minute when she ran off and phoned you."

Joan smiled. "That's Carmel all right. She's always doing things like that. Would you like some tea?"

"If you have some of your mother's porter cake to go with it. Carmel told me about it."

Joan laughed. "That one! Would you like some homemade butter on it?"

"From your farm in County Galway?"

Joan smiled. "I was at home last weekend. My mother always loads me up before I come back to Dublin."

While I was drinking the tea and eating the cake, I glanced around the room. "It must be nearly two months since I was here last?"

"Three actually." Joan turned down the volume of the radio and sat in an armchair opposite me.

"You have a good memory. I meant to write to you, but I had a lot of trouble with the band when we went back to England that time. I'm solo now."

Joan ran her finger through her hair. "You don't need to apologise. We only went out together that one time."

I swallowed some cake. "Yeah, but I wouldn't like you getting the wrong impression. I really enjoyed being with you. I tried to write a song about you in Killala."

Joan flicked back her hair. "I'm sure you did!"

"Honest."

She looked down at her bare knees and glanced at the radio. Emmylou Harris was singing 'Here, There and Everywhere'. I put down my cup and went over and took her hands. She stood up. We started kissing.

THE KNOWLEDGE

In my reckless career I've been a fool and a sinner
ON THE WATER

E D'S MOTHER OPENED the front door and smiled. "Johnny. Come in. He's still in bed, wouldn't you know. I'll call him. You can wait in the kitchen."

I left my guitar case in the hall and went and sat in the kitchen. A few moments later, Mrs Deane came into the room shaking her head. "He'd sleep all day, if I didn't call him."

She buttered some bread, grated cheese on top of it and put it under the grill. Then she looked at her watch. "I bet he's gone back to sleep. I'd better call him again; I have to leave soon."

Soon after she returned to the kitchen, Ed came into the room yawning and scratching his head. With his eyes lowered, he gave me a hint of a smile and then started sniffing the air, making crooked faces at his mother. "I hope the toast isn't going to be burnt again. You know I hate it when the cheese gets all hard and crusty. You'd better take it up."

Mrs Deane shook her head and started to leave the room. "Take it up yourself. I have to be in town in ten minute. Goodbye, Johnny."

"Good luck, Mrs Deane."

Ed poured me a mug of coffee, then took up his breakfast and sat at the table jabbing at the burnt cheese with a knife. "I really hate burnt toast!"

I smiled to myself, trying to think of a topic of conversation that might take his mind of his tragedy. "Was I telling you I ran into Peters in Grafton Street at the weekend? Hadn't seen him since I parted from the band. He was telling me Jim and himself are thinking of going to a festival in India for some guru."

Ed swallowed some toast. "They started getting into him before the band broke up. They got the knowledge in some ashram in Hampstead."

"What knowledge is that?"

Ed grinned. "Don't ask me! You have to get it before you can fully understand what it is, apparently. And you have to be in the right frame of mind before they'll give it to you in the first place."

"Sounds pretty strange."

Ed shrugged. "All religion is strange, if you ask me. I was educated by priests at Belvedere College. They were fairly liberal, but some of them were still very peculiar."

I swallowed some coffee. "I didn't know you went to Belvedere. Joyce was educated there, wasn't it? I read *Portrait of the Artist* recently."

Ed swallowed some toast. "I must read it myself sometime."

"I got it mainly to see how he lost his faith. I'm surprised Peters gave up his; he was always a very devout Catholic."

Ed shrugged and drank some coffee. "Must have been difficult for you meeting him after the way you parted from the band."

"Not really. I never hold grudges."

Ed ate in silence for a few moments, then pushed the plate of half-eaten toast to the centre of the table and stood up. "How many more songs do you want to practice for the session?"

"Two or three. I've asked Kevin to come along to put some keyboards on a few of the tracks. He's quick; he'll have no bother learning them. I need to have the mixes ready before Monday week. That's when I go to London."

Ed lit a cigarette. "Before we start, I'd like to play you a track or two of a new album by Captain Beefheart. It's really interesting."

We went to Ed's room. The place was a total mess, with clothes, books and record albums scattered all over the bed and floor. Ed rummaged through some records and found the one he was looking for. While he was putting it on, I sat on the edge of his unmade bed and took up a book lying near the pillow. It was a biography of Marcel Duchamp. I flicked through some pages, glancing at pictures and reading snatches of text.

The record started to play. Strange dissonant sounds began to fill the room; then a deep baritone voice started singing like a truculent old black man. Ed glanced at me with a wry smile, waiting for my reaction. The combination of his crooked facial expression and the Negro-like voice in the background reminded me of an incident from when we were both still in the band together. We were listening to an album by an old blues singer while under the influence of LSD, and both of us began to laugh at the moaning sound of the old voice. While we were laughing, I looked into Ed's face and saw some of my own facial features in his expression, as though I was looking at myself in a mirror. I realised I was hallucinating but still felt uneasy at the thought of what we were doing. "I don't think we should be laughing like this, should we? The poor old guy sounds like he's really in pain." Ed lowered his eyes. "You're right. It's just that I've grown a bit cynical about the blues lately. There's so much hype about it everywhere."

Ed glanced towers his stereo unit. "What do you think of the Captain?"

I shrugged. "Almost as authentic as the real thing, but I'm getting a bit tired of white singers copying blacks, including myself." I raised the book in my hand. "Who's this Duchamp fella?"

"A French artist. Anti-artist, actually. He has some interesting ideas. Did you see his *Mona Lisa*?"

I laughed "His *Mona Lisa*?! The only thing that's his is the moustache."

Ed grinned. "It's supposed to be ironic. What are you reading yourself these days?"

I put the book back by the pillow. "*The History of Philosophy* by Bertrand Russell and some of the Russian writers."

One track of the album ended and another began. This one sounded even more brash than the first number. Ed saw that I wasn't enjoying it so he took it off. "Like everything else, musical taste is just convention. We familiarise ourselves with arrangements of notes and get used to the patterns for a while. Then we tire of them, and new arrangements are found to fill the vacuum."

"Sounds very cynical. You don't believe that, do you?"

Ed hunched his shoulders. "Sometimes. We'd better get down to work on your songs. My amp's set up in the living room."

The living room was cluttered up with dark antique furniture. Ed's amplifier looked completely out of place sitting in front of a chaise longue. To the left of the amp, an old upright piano stood against a wall with a row of gilt-framed family portraits on top of it. While Ed was plugging in his electric guitar and regulating the controls, I went and looked at one of the photos. It was a shot of a pilot standing by the propeller of a small, twin-engine plane. "Who's the pilot?"

Ed looked up from his guitar. "My father."

"Flies, does he?"

"Used to. He was very proud of that plane, a Swallow. A friend of his crashed it while my father was teaching him to fly. They were both lucky to come out alive. The friend – who caused the crash – escaped with hardly a bruise, but my father broke both his legs on impact. It was in all the papers at the time."

I shook my head. "You don't often hear of people surviving plane crashes. Where's your father now?"

Ed hesitated. "England. While he was recuperating in hospital, his construction business went bust. We had to sell our house in leafy Rathmines and move into this little place. Then my father had to leave Ireland to find work. He's been living in England for some years. I visited him a few times while I was in London with the band. He's thinking of coming home soon."

I looked at the photo again. "I witnessed a plane crash when I was nine or ten. A glider it was. It was taking part in air display above Limerick, and one of its wings clipped the wing of another glider during a manoeuvre. The pilot tried to land on the site of a grotto, but there were children playing around the statue of Our Lady. To avoid them, he crashed right into the gable end of a house. Killed instantly he was. There's was nothing left of the plane; just matchwood. I've often thought about that split second when he decided to sacrifice his own life for the lives of those kids. It was a brave thing to do."

Ed lowered his eyes. "My father was lucky; he crash-landed in a field. Came out of it with a few broken bones, but the plane was a complete write-off."

I shook my head. "An amazing story."

Ed shrugged and turned his attention back to his guitar. "We better get in tune with one another and get on with it."

While I was tuning my strings, Ed suddenly turned up the volume of his Stratocaster to maximum level and started slashing at it for no apparent reason. A loud wail of feedback went up from his amplifier. Automatically I stuck my fingers in my ears and made a crooked face. Ed stopped the noise and grinned. "Sorry about that; I just get this mad urge to out-do Hendrix sometimes. Go on, start playing one of your songs. I'll follow you."

I started singing. Ed listened for the duration of a verse, then nodded. "Nice melody. Reminds me of something, but I can't remember what."

This remark bothered me, but I kept singing. Ed began to play along with me. The pure tone of some of the runs he started coming up with bolstered the words I was singing and carried the melody along effort-lessly. After the first chorus, I smiled to myself at the ease of his playing. His head was bent over the curve of his guitar, so he didn't notice the pleasure he was giving me. As we neared the end of the song, I recalled the cynical remarks he had made earlier about music, and smiled to myself.

We ran over the song three or four times and started working on another number. In the middle of our first run-through, the room door opened and a raven-haired girl of fifteen or sixteen looked in at us with a big bright smile on her face. "Don't mind me, keep going. You sound great." She listened for a few moments, then smiled again and closed the door. When the song came to an end, I looked at Ed. "Your sister? She looks just like you, except for the smile."

Ed grinned. "Yeah, very funny."

We went on practising for a couple of hours; then Ed decided to walk into town with me to pass away the afternoon. When we reached the city centre, I suggested browsing around some of the bookshops. We made our way to Dawson Street and went into one. At Ed's suggestion, we made our way to the art and painting section. Ed took down a book on surreal-ism and started looking through it while I flicked through an anthology of impressionist paintings. I came on a picture called *Misty Morning at Creil* by Pissarro. The delicate tones and tints of the misty landscape took my breath away. I showed the painting to Ed. He glanced at the cover of the book and grinned. "Paintings for chocolate boxes."

"I think it's a terrific picture." I looked at it again. There was very little substance in it apart from a few strokes of paint indicating human, animal and tree forms, and yet it was radiant with life. "I have to get this. Here, hold my guitar."

Ed took the case from me. "That's an expensive book."

I glanced round the shop and then slipped the volume quickly inside the front of my jacket, gripping it under my arm. My blood started to race. Ed looked at me askance. "Jesus, what are you doing? You'll be caught!"

"No, I won't. I know exactly where the security mirrors are."

Ed looked nervously over his shoulder. "Let's get out of here fast."

"Hang on. I may as well be hung for a sheep as a lamb. Let's go down to the literary section."

Ed hesitated, then followed me to the Penguin shelves. After scanning one or two rows of novels, I picked up *Dead Souls* by Gogol. "This guy's short stories are terrific. I've been meaning to get this one for a long time." I stepped out of the range of an overhead mirror and glanced round the shop. When I was sure there was no one looking, I slipped the paperback under my free arm and told Ed to head out. While we were leaving the shop, a rush of adrenaline ran through my veins as though I was walking a tightrope. After we got outside and took a few steps away from the front door, I let out a sigh of relief.

Ed looked at me and shook his head. "You're an awful chancer!"

We made our way to the top of Grafton Street. I glanced across at the front gate of St Stephen's Green. "I'm meeting Joan there in thirty minutes or so. We're going to the pictures."

Ed took some small change from his pocket. "I may as well catch a bus home. I've enough exercise for one day. See you Friday morning at the studio."

"I'll phone you to make sure you're up on time."

Crossing the street, Ed glanced back at me and shook his head and laughed.

I walked across to the green and spent thirty minutes sitting on a bench by the pond browsing through the stolen books, then put them in my guitar case and made my way to the main gate. While I was standing there a memory from the distant past came back to me. My sister Pattie arrived home one day full of excitement because she'd found a five pound note on the floor of a local shop. While she was speculating on what sweets she was going to buy with the windfall, my father arrived home from work and immediately made her take the money back to the shop and hand it over to the assistant. "Never take or keep anything that doesn't belong to you!"

An old man passing by glanced at me. I lowered my eyes. When I looked up again, Joan was coming towards me on the pavement. When she spotted me, her face lit up with a pure smile. I switched the guitar case from one hand to the other and went to meet her.

TED'S VINTAGE ROCK'N'ROLL LIBRARY

This time he feels he'll have success
He feels it in his bones
THIS TIME

B RENDA LEE WOKE me at dawn, purring on the windowsill beside the bed, waiting to be let out. Though I was annoyed at being woken so early, I was used to it after four days of staying in Ted's flat. A provision of being loaned the place for the week I was in London was that I had to feed the cat twice a day and open the window whenever she wanted to go outside. Before jetting off to attend a series of vintage rock'n'roll record auctions around Europe, Ted (an old friend) had warned me that Brenda was liable to piss all over the room if she wasn't let out at least twice a day, but he hadn't mentioned that I would have to get up at six o'clock in the morning to do it.

After I let the cat out, I couldn't get back to sleep. I lay on my pillow looking around at the shelves of old records that covered almost every inch of visible space in the room. The only part of the bedsit that wasn't overshadowed by old vinyl was the kitchenette and the bed I was lying in. Ted ran his own mail-order business, and he also had a small record shop in Camden Town that specialised in vintage rock'n'roll.

I leaned across to the chair beside the bed and picked up a paperback copy of *Thus Spake Zarathustra* by Nietzsche, a book I had brought with me from Dublin to instil courage and determination in myself for the godless task of doing the rounds of the record companies in search of a recording deal. In the three weary days I had spent traipsing from company to company with my demos, I had managed to inveigle my way into five A&R offices. Four of the A&R men I spoke to gave my tape a careful listen but turned me down on the grounds that my songs weren't commercial. The fifth, a top scout at Elton John's newly established Rocket Records, didn't have time to give my tape immediate attention but phoned me the morning after I left it with him, full of enthusiasm for my voice and songs. He told me that he was putting in a strong recommendation that the company sign me to a long-term contract. "Call to the office on Friday afternoon between four and five, and I'll have a definitive answer for you."

This appointment (made a couple of mornings earlier) had kept my spirits high during the previous days, but now that Friday had arrived apprehension began to set in.

I read in bed for a few hours to try and distract myself, then got up and dressed. While I was having breakfast, Brenda Lee came back to the window and started clawing at the glass. I let her in and gave her some Kit-e-Kat and a bowl of milk.

After breakfast, I caught a tube down to Charing Cross and browsed around Foyles bookshop for an hour. Then I made my way to Trafalgar Square and passed another couple of hours in the National Gallery. At around one-thirty, I strolled up to Piccadilly Circus and had lunch in a sandwich bar. I arrived at Rocket Records just after three, almost an hour before my scheduled time to be there. To pass more time, I strolled down to Oxford Street and was back at Rocket Records at twenty minutes to four. I stood outside the building for ten minutes, then pushed open the door and went upstairs. A dark-haired receptionist phoned my name through to the A&R department and asked me to take a seat.

While I was waiting in the reception area, Elton John emerged from an office across from where I was sitting with two members of his band. The three of them sat for a moment in conversation; then Elton stood up and started pacing the floor awkwardly in a pair of high platform boots.

He looked troubled, as though he was just after hearing bad news. While I was watching him – and wondering what a millionaire with a string of hit albums under his belt would have cause to worry about – the A&R man I had the appointment with came out of another office and walked over and sat beside me. He had my tape in his hand and he wasn't smiling.

"I'm sorry for keeping you, mate, but it's been hectic here all day. I'm not going to beat about the bush; I haven't time. It's been decided that we have enough acts on our roster for the time being, so we're going to have to pass on you. I'm sorry about this. I tried my best to convince them that you have something special, but there was nothing I could do." He got to his feet and handed me the demo tape. "You might try sending me some more material at a future date. By then things might have changed. I wish I had more time to talk to you now, but I'm up to my eyes. Good luck to you, mate."

Before I had a chance to say anything, the A&R man disappeared back into his office. I sat for a few seconds crestfallen, then slowly got to my feet. Elton John was still pacing the floor in front of me in his high silver shoes. For a moment I thought of walking over to him and asking him to give my demos a listen. I looked at the tape in my hand and took a deep breath. At that moment, Elton turned towards me and gave me a sullen look. I put the tape in my pocket and left the office.

I trudged back to Trafalgar Square and sat on a bench beside an old man feeding pigeons. I started thinking of Joan back in Dublin. During a phone call to her the night before, I had promised to ring again after the meeting I'd just come from. But now, as I gazed at the pigeons pecking breadcrumbs from the ground in front of me, I didn't have the heart to call her. A surge of self-pity rose up inside me. Tears came to my eyes and everything became blurred. A passer-by glanced at me. I pulled myself together, stood up and made my way to Charing Cross tube station.

The train was packed with Friday evening commuters, many of them laughing and joking, getting into the free weekend spirit. During the journey, I decided I couldn't face the loneliness of Ted's flat in my present condition, so I got off the tube at Swiss Cottage and made my way to the Swiss Cottage Inn. Though it was just after six when I arrived there, the place was half full. I bought myself a double whiskey and a pint of beer in one of the main chalet-style bars and sat in an empty corner. I drank back the whiskey in two quick gulps and brooded over the beer. Half an hour later I ordered the same again. By nine-thirty the bar was full, and I was plastered. I swayed up to the counter for one last pint, but the bartender wouldn't serve me. "Go home, you're drunk."

I jostled my way through the tightly packed crowd to one of the other bars and ordered a pint of lager from a barman wearing a heavy pair of spectacles. He squinted through his thick lenses but served me the drink.

While I was polishing off this last beer, the bar room went into a spin and I almost toppled over. I lit a cigarette and stumbled out the door.

Without looking either left or right, I started crossing a wide street. A passing car swerved to avoid me and beeped its horn. I laughed and started singing one of the songs from my rejected demo tape: *Changing space, always moving. Nothing ever stays for very long. . .*

When I arrived at Ted's place, I fell in the front door and crawled along the hall to the room. With great effort, I managed to get to my feet and insert the key in the lock. Inside the flat, I stumbled across the room without turning on the light and collapsed on to the end of the bed. Brenda Lee started purring somewhere in the dark. I shook my head, unable to get to my feet to open the window to let her out. I dragged myself up to the pillow and pulled some blankets over my back. I felt a terrible urge to go to the toilet but didn't have the energy to get off the bed. I passed out.

Sometime in the middle of the night, I woke up drenched to the skin in my own warm piss. I groaned heavily and went back to sleep. A few hours later I woke again. The cat was sitting on the windowsill purring like mad to get out. By now it was bright, and the piss I was lying in had turned stone cold. I cursed into the pillow and dragged myself off the bed. I was saturated.

I drew back the covers and sheets to see the damage. The wet stain on the mattress wasn't as bad as I imagined it was going be. The blankets and sheets and my own clothes had absorbed most of the piss.

I stripped out of my wet things and put on some dry clothes; then I stuffed the sheets and blankets into a plastic bag and set them aside to take to the laundrette later in the day. I dragged the mattress from the bed and put it in front of the electric fire to dry. While I was doing this, Brenda

Lee remained on the windowsill, purring and clawing at the glass. When I finally got round to opening the window for her, she was gone, and a yellow pool of piss was dripping from the sill on to the floor. I cursed and went to get a cloth from the kitchen.

After I mopped up the cat's piss, I flopped into an armchair and closed my eyes. Despite a pounding headache and a churning stomach, I fell asleep with my head on the wooden arm of the chair.

A smell of burning cloth woke me. I jumped up from the armchair and kicked the mattress away from the front of the electric fire. Luckily it wasn't in flames, but the brown outline of an ugly scorch mark was indelibly printed on the striped material. Cursing myself, I opened the window to let out the smell of burnt piss and then returned to the armchair and tried to go back to sleep.

Brenda Lee started purring again. I opened my eyes and noticed that she was walking up and down outside the kitchenette with her tail in the air. Watching her, it dawned on me that I hadn't fed her her second meal the day before. I hopped up and gave her some Kit-e-Kat and a bowl of milk. Then I collapsed back into the armchair and closed my eyes. An attack of hiccups kept me from sleeping. I sat up in the armchair, belching and cursing.

In the half-light of dawn, the room appeared narrower than it normally looked. I gazed around the shelves of old records and began to feel like I was entombed in a crypt. I stretched out my hand and took down a few albums. I didn't recognise any of the bequiffed musicians on the covers. Neither was I familiar with any of the song titles on the backs of the album sleeves. I switched on Ted's record player and played portions of songs from a few of the records. They all sounded pretty much the same. I looked around the shelves again and calculated that there were thousands of other mediocre songs that I'd never heard among the collection. I shuddered at the thought.

I hopped up and got my demo tape from the pocket of my wet jacket. The inlay card with the list of song titles was wet at the edges. I took the tape out of the plastic case and placed it in Ted's cassette player and turned it on. My own voice began to sing: *Changing space always moving, nothing ever stays for very long. Changing minds for these changing times, nothing ever stays in one place. . .*

I started hearing echoes of other songwriters' melodies in the tune. Even my voice sounded unnatural and contrived. The whole production was false and derivative. I couldn't listen to it. I knocked off the cassette player and sat back in the armchair holding my head. On the rug in front of me, Brenda Lee was licking the curved talons of one of her paws. I watched her for a few moments; then I put my face into my open hands and wept.

IN DEEP

Ballybunion here we come
FOURTH SKIN BLUES

THE FRONT OF the car had gone right through the low stone wall and was partly suspended over a drop of thirty feet or more. Beside me in the back seat, Joan was trembling and her face was as white as a sheet. Though I had let out a loud roar just before the car hit the wall, I felt surprisingly calm. I put my arm around Joan's shoulder and took her hand. "We're OK; we didn't go over. We're safe."

The woman in the front passenger seat opened her safety belt and put her hand on the driver's arm. "Are you all right, Tom?"

The driver took a deep breath. "I'm fine, Marge. I just got a shock, that's all. I wasn't expecting the bend to be so sharp. These goddamn Irish roads!"

He raised himself in his seat and looked out at the deep drop beyond the front of the hood. "My God, take a look at that, Marge!"

Marge looked out and gasped. "Gee!"

The driver glanced back at me and shook his head. "Are you two all right back there?"

"We're fine."

We all got out of the car and looked down at the rocky gorge. Joan shook her head and gave a nervous laugh. "We're lucky we didn't go over, aren't we?"

The driver scratched his head. "I don't know how it happened. I just took my eyes off the wheel for a moment and bang! We're not used to these narrow roads back in the States, are we, Marge?"

Marge shook her head and smiled at Joan. "I bet you two are sorry you took the ride with us now?"

The driver looked at me. "And to think you only got into the car at the bottom of the hill!"

I nodded. "Accidents happen."

Surprisingly, little damage had been done to the vehicle. One side of the fender was dented and the left headlight was smashed, but when we pushed the car back into the centre of the road, the engine started up straightaway.

The driver kept well below forty miles an hour during the rest of the journey.

While we were driving along the winding Kerry road, Marge looked over her shoulder. "I hope you guys aren't in a hurry? At this rate we won't get to Listowel till nightfall."

I smiled. "We're in no rush. We're on a camping holiday, just drifting around. We plan to stay in a place called Ballybunion for the next few days. It's by the sea, not too far from Listowel."

The driver glanced back at the guitar case leaning against the haversack on the seat beside me. "I was just about to ask you before we had the mishap, what kind of music do you play?"

"Modern folk music, I suppose you'd call it. I write my own songs."

"Gee, that must be satisfying."

Marge turned to Joan. "And what do you do, honey? Sing?"

Joan laughed. "I haven't a note in my head. I'm a schoolteacher."

We parted company from the couple in Listowel and were lucky enough to catch the last bus to Ballybunion almost straightaway.

The sun was going down when we arrived in the small coastal town. We pitched our tent in a field near some cliffs overlooking Nuns' Cove, a spot I was familiar with from family day trips to the place many years before. After we settled our things in the tent, we walked back to town and had a meal of fish and chips in a cheap restaurant, then went to a bar for a drink.

Halfway through my beer, a terrible sense of claustrophobia came over me, even though the bar was half empty. Joan noticed the queasy look on my face. "What's wrong? You look very pale."

"I don't know. I just feel kind of strange all of a sudden."

I looked across at some customers talking and laughing by the counter. Everything seemed normal, yet I was filled with an awful sense of foreboding, as though something terrible was about to happen. For Joan's sake, I tried to pull myself together, but the oppressive feeling grew worse. I hopped up from my chair. "I'm going outside to get some fresh air. I'll be back in a few minutes."

A look of alarm came over Joan's face. "I'll come with you."

"No, no, you stay here and mind the drinks. I'll be back in a little while."

Outside the bar, I took a few deep breaths but didn't feel any better. I made my way along the narrow street as far as the seafront and sat on a bench in an isolated spot on an embankment overlooking the sea. The sound of breakers crashing on the dark beach down below made me forget myself for a few moments, but then the feeling of dread returned. I looked out over the black ocean and started to shiver. The pressure in my head grew so intense I began to groan under my breath. While I was doing this, the thought struck me that the panic attack I was experiencing might in some way be connected to my mother's mental illness. I began to rock backwards and forwards, terrified by the idea that I might be having a nervous breakdown. I started crying, gently at first, but then a more violent bout of sobbing overtook me.

A distant light beaming intermittently across the dark skyline caught my attention. I watched it for a while. It appeared to be a lighthouse or a beacon tower over on the Clare coast. Between one revolving beam and the next there was a regular gap of five or six seconds. While I was measuring the time, I remembered a game I used to play with my sisters of counting car lights on our bedroom ceiling when we were young. The game, I recalled, helped us relax and go to sleep. Remembering this now calmed me down. I went on watching the beam till eventually I began to feel better. I wiped my eyes and took a few deep breaths of the salty air;

then I stood up and walked over to a safety rail at the edge of the embankment. White breakers were just about visible in the darkness down below. I watched them curling on to the beach for a few moments; then I thought of Joan and hurried back to the bar.

Joan stood up as I approached the table. "Where were you? I was worried stiff. I went outside but I couldn't see you anywhere?"

I took her hand. "I'm sorry I was so long. I went to the seafront to clear my head. I'm a bit better now."

"You still look a bit shaky."

"I'm fine, really. I'm just tired, that's all. Do you mind if we go?"

Joan looked down at my glass of beer. "Are you not going to finish your drink?"

"I don't feel like it. I'm exhausted."

Back at the tent, I fell asleep the moment my head hit the ground.

The sound of gulls squealing and waves breaking woke me at dawn. Joan was fast asleep beside me. I slipped out of the sleeping bag without waking her and put on my jeans.

Outside the grass was wet with dew. In my bare feet I made my way to the edge of the cliff and looked down at Nuns' Cove. In the middle of the rocky inlet, gulls were gliding above a huge escarpment of rock jutting out of the water. The sight took my breath away. I sat on a stone and looked out over the ocean. The sky above the sea was tinged with a light pink hue. I glanced over my shoulder at the rising sun on the eastern horizon. It appeared to be pulsating like a living heart. Watching it, my own heart rose up inside me. I turned back to the sea.

While my eyes were drifting over the Atlantic, I remembered the panic attack of the night before and came to the conclusion that it had been triggered off by a delayed reaction to the car crash earlier in the day. I recalled the childhood car-light game that the beacon light had brought back to me at the height of the crisis. While I was thinking about the relief that the old memory had given me, a recent melody I'd written came into my head, and a few lines formed around it without any effort on my part: *Sister, we're alone in the middle of the night, counting car lights on the ceiling, everything will be all right.* Despite the early hour, I rushed back to the tent and got my guitar and song copybook. I returned to the rock near the cliff edge, and, within the space of an hour, I had a full song written:

Sister, we're alone in the middle of the night
Counting car lights on the ceiling
Everything will be all right
Mother had a breakdown, that's 'cause she was sad
Let's just count the car lights, mother isn't mad
Mother isn't mad, she's just sad
Mother isn't mad, I tell you, and father isn't bad
Sister, stop your crying, why can't you play the game
The lights coming from the left are yours
The ones from the right I claim
Sister, stop your crying, all old people are the same
It happens to them all, Bobby told me
His mother's just the same

Just as I was completing the final verse, Joan stuck her head out of the tent and smiled up at me. "You're at it early enough! I heard you singing awhile back, but I thought I was dreaming."

I picked up the copybook and went towards her. "I have a new song written. Will I sing it for you?"

Joan looked at her watch and laughed. "It's not even half seven. I don't know what my critical faculties will be like at this hour, but go ahead."

I sat on the grass outside the tent and sang the song. When I finished it, Joan took a deep breath. "I don't know what to say. It's very sad. Did it really happen?"

"In a way. My mother suffers from manic depression. She's suffered with it most of her adult life."

Joan brushed a strand of hair out of her eye. "You certainly capture the feeling of sadness. But do you think you should sing about such things?"

I thought for a moment. "I'm not sure. I don't know if I'd ever sing it in public, but I felt I had to write it. In a way, it wrote itself."

I moved into the tent and put my arms around Joan's waist. "I always feel great after writing a song, no matter how sad the lyric is. Strange, isn't it?"

Joan smiled. "Must be the sense of achievement."

"Relief would be more like it. By the way, I'm sorry about last night. I don't know what came over me. Maybe it was the song building up inside me."

I looked into Joan's eyes. Some freckles had appeared around her nose during the previous sunny days, giving her face a schoolgirl look. She was kneeling on the blue sleeping bag with her head tilted slightly to one side. Her white bra and panties were showing up the deep tone of her tan. We started kissing. A gull cried out above the tent. I became aware of the sound of waves crashing in the nearby cove. I touched one of the freckles above Joan's high cheekbone. "Let's go down to the shore, and I'll teach you to swim."

Joan smiled nervously. "I told you before, I'm afraid of the water."

"Come on, there'll be no one there at this time. We'll have it all to ourselves."

On the pebbled beach, we left our towels on a rock and ran to the edge of the water. A wave broke over our feet. Joan hunched her shoulders and shivered. "It's cold. I don't think I'll go in."

"Come on; it'll be nice once we're inside." I took her hand and led her out into the blue foaming water till we were in above our waists. A wave came hurtling towards us. Joan gasped and tried to pull away from me, but I held her back. The wave crashed against our bodies, and white foam bubbled and frothed around us. I let go of Joan's hand and ducked beneath the surf. When I resurfaced, I noticed that Joan's tanned breasts were heaving above her blue bikini top. A sharp thrill rose up inside me. I put my arms around her waist and pressed up against her. "There's no need to be afraid. If you want to learn how to swim, you have to come out this far."

Another high wave crashed against us. Joan clung closer to me. "I've never been in this deep before. I'm frightened."

I lowered my hands to her hips and kissed her neck. "I warned you when you teamed up with me that you were getting in over your head."

THE BREWERY

I risked my soul to be a winner
ON THE WATER

I WAS READING in bed in the exposed loft above the kitchen-dining
room when Oscar's sons, Fintan and Mark, came running into the
room followed by their mother, Naomi.

"Be quiet boys, you'll wake Johnny. Fintan, get out the cereal
bowls, and you, Mark, get the spoons. Hurry along now; you're late for
school as it is."

I moved back into the shadows and pretended to be asleep, but I could
still see part of what was going on down in the dining area.

A row broke out between the two boys at the kitchen table. Mark, the
younger of the two, didn't like the bowl his brother gave him. "That's not
my bowl! You have my bowl. I won't eat out of this pinky one."

"That's not pink, you old baby. That's white."

Naomi drew a loud breath. "Give him the yellow bowl, Fintan. You
know well that that's his bowl. Why do you always have to be so
difficult?"

"Why does he always get his own way? Now I'm going to have to take
out my Weetabix, and then you'll be giving out to me for putting crumbs
all over the table."

"I want my bowl! I want my bowl!"

"I'm giving it to you, you old baby!"

While they were eating, Fintan looked up at the loft. "Will that man be staying here for long, Mummy?"

Naomi put her finger to her mouth. "Shhhh. I told you yesterday, he'll only be here for a few days – like the last time – till he and Daddy record some songs. Now hurry on and eat up."

After Naomi and the children left the house, I picked up my book and went on reading. Twenty or thirty minutes went by. Then the kitchen door opened again and Oscar came into the room with the morning post in his hand, smoking a cigarette and coughing. He stubbed the cigarette out in an ashtray on the kitchen table and looked up at the loft. "Hey, Johnny, are you awake up there?"

I leaned out of the bed. "Good morning, Oscar. Yeah, I'm just doing a bit of reading."

Oscar started filling the kettle. "You read a lot. I noticed it when you were here for the audition a few weeks back. What book are you reading?"

I hesitated. "*The Origins of Species*."

Oscar raised his eyebrows. "Not exactly light stuff you go in for, is it?"

"I'm just curious to know where the hair on my toes comes from."

Oscar laughed. "I feel pretty hairy myself this morning after the dope I smoked when we got in from the pub last night. I envy you your self-control. You only had a couple of pints in the bar, too, I noticed. Very abstemious, aren't you?"

I started getting out of bed. "I get pains in my stomach if I drink too much. I think I might be developing ulcers."

Oscar laughed. "I've had them for years, but that never stopped me from having my jar."

I dressed and climbed down the narrow wooden ladder into the kitchen. "I really like this open-plan arrangement you have here. It's a bit like sleeping in the galley of a ship."

Oscar glanced up at the loft. "We were stuck for a spare room, so we converted it last year. We were going to wall it off and put in some proper steps, but we ran out of funds."

"I'd leave it the way it is. It has more character like that."

Oscar pointed to a press. "Help yourself to some cereal. You know where everything is."

222

I filled myself a bowl of Weetabix and sat at the table, eating. When the kettle boiled, Oscar tipped the equivalent of four spoons of instant coffee into a mug and poured boiling water in on top of it. "This should get my motor going."

"You don't eat very much, I've noticed. A bad appetite, have you?"

Oscar sat in a chair opposite me, sipping his coffee. "I never touch solids at this time of the day. I usually have a bite at lunchtime and eat something proper in the evenings." He lit a cigarette and opened one of the letters.

I looked around the room. A framed photograph of an old abandoned car on the wall beside the delph cabinet caught my attention. I went over and took a close look at it, then returned to my chair. "That's a really nice photograph, the way the sun is framed in the window of the car. I didn't notice it the last time I was here."

Oscar glanced at the photograph. "Did I not tell you, I was a professional photographer before I started the Brewery? I took that one back in Dublin when I was starting out in the early sixties. When I came to London and got married, I sacrificed my art for a comfortable lifestyle. I ended up doing a lot of commercial work for magazines and brochures. Boring stuff, but it paid well."

I looked back at the photograph. "You were a fine photographer."

Oscar waved his hand dismissively. "I prefer music. I always wanted to become a professional musician, but I didn't have the nerve for it when I was younger."

I looked at Oscar's bony face. The skin around his eyes and cheekbones was drooping like melted wax. He looked like an old man, though I had been told he was only in his mid-thirties.

After he read a few lines of his letter, he threw it on the table and cursed. "Another bank warning. That's the second this week. The one thing I miss about photography is the steady income. I'm going to have to do some more juggling with my accounts."

"Juggling?"

Oscar gulped back some coffee. "Borrowing from one bank to pay back another. I do it all the time. I have to. The mortgage on this house alone is colossal, and we also have a cottage in the country. We bought it last year for a song, but the renovations are costing a fortune. It's held up at present because of lack of resources. As soon as the record deal comes through, I'll finish it with some of the advance money. It'll be a great place for practising for the band."

"You seem very sure you'll get the deal?"

"Positive. The only reason A&M held off in the past was because we were weak vocally. Now that you're on board, we'll have no problems."

Oscar finished his coffee and got to his feet. "Will we go to the studio? I have this new song I'd like you to try. It's called 'Impatient'. It would be great to have it arranged for when the band arrive in the afternoon."

I followed Oscar to a small soundproofed room at the front of the house. It was full of amplifiers and musical instruments. Oscar switched on an electric piano and settled a copybook on top of it. He played around with some chords for a few moments; then he cleared his throat and started singing in a shaky, high-pitched voice: *I'm impatient, I can't go slow. I'm impatient, I can't wait to go. I get up in the morning and. . .*

I shifted on the edge of a chair, trying not to let the boredom I was feeling show on my face. When the song came to an end, Oscar started fumbling in his pockets for his cigarettes. "It might need a bit more work on the chorus, but that's it basically. What do you think?"

I rubbed my neck. "The range might be a bit of a problem for me. Maybe you should sing this one yourself."

Oscar's face dropped. "You didn't like it?"

"It isn't that. I just don't think it would suit the way I sing."

"I could change the key."

"It's not just the key. That twelve bar rock'n'roll style that you're so good at doesn't really work for me."

Oscar looked at me suspiciously. "But when you agreed to join the band, it was on the basis that you'd sing my songs as well as your own."

"Yeah, but only if your songs suit me." I shifted uneasily on my chair, knowing full well that I hadn't included any such stipulation when I had accepted the job.

Oscar lit a cigarette and played a few chords on the keyboard. "Maybe if I change the structure a little it might suit you better. Here, let me try a few things."

For twenty or thirty minutes, Oscar turned his song inside out in a desperate attempt to make it more suitable for me. The final arrangement he settled on didn't sound much better than the original version, but I sang it, half-heartedly, nonetheless. When I reached the chorus, Oscar tried to sing a harmony line with me and ended up breaking into a fit of coughing. His face turned purple. He stopped playing the piano and stumbled around the room in near convulsions. When he got his breath back, he returned to the piano and looked at me. "I'll have to give up them damned fags or they'll kill me. What do you think of the song now? You certainly make a better job of singing it than I do."

I hesitated. "I find it a bit of a strain, to be quite honest with you."

Oscar lowered his eyes. "We'll come back to it later. Maybe you'd like to try one of your own songs?"

"If you like."

I got my guitar and started singing a ballad called "Another Time, Another Place". When I reached the chorus, Oscar took a clarinet from the top of the piano and started improvising a counter melody to the air I was singing. At the end of the song, he nodded and smiled. "That was really nice. There's almost a classical feel to it. It's even better than the song you played at the audition. Where do you get them melodies from?"

I sat up. "I listen to a lot of classical music – Chopin, Satie, Beethoven, that type of stuff. Maybe that's where the influence comes from."

Oscar lit a cigarette. "Whatever formula you've got, it works. Will we do it again? This time I'll try doing a clarinet intro using the chorus melody, if that's OK?"

"Fine."

We were still arranging the number an hour later when Naomi arrived home. She tiptoed into the studio with a plastic carrier bag in her hand and stood listening to the song. When it came to an end, she looked at me and smiled. "Very nice. Is that a new one?"

"I wrote it over a year ago."

Oscar put down the clarinet and lit a cigarette. "It should work a treat with the band."

Naomi turned to Oscar. "I'm sorry I'm so late. I called to see Viv on the way back from the shops and I couldn't get away from her. Ron's left her again. She thinks it's for good this time. But I'll tell you about it later. I'll let you get on with your work. Would you like some coffee?"

Oscar took a deep pull from his cigarette. "I think we'll go round to the

Crows' Nest for a bit of early lunch. That way we'll have the full afternoon for the rehearsal with the band."

Naomi looked at her watch. "But it's not even twelve o'clock yet?"

Oscar shrugged. "So what? We can get some toasted sandwiches. I'm sure Johnny would like a snack before the band arrive."

I scratched my ear. "I don't mind. We can have something here, if you like."

Naomi raised her plastic bag. "I got some fresh cheese and tomatoes at Tesco. I won't be a minute making some sandwiches."

Oscar stubbed out his cigarette. "Don't bother. We need to get out of the house for a while. We've been working all morning. You can stay here if you like."

Naomi looked at Oscar. "No, I'll go with you. Just give me a minute to put these things away."

At the Crows' Nest, Oscar ordered a couple of toasted cheese sandwiches, two mugs of coffee and a pint of lager. When the order arrived, he placed the sandwiches in front of Naomi and me and put the beer on a mat in front of himself. Naomi looked at him. "I thought this sandwich was for you?"

"I'm not hungry."

Naomi took half of the sandwich from the plate. "Here, we'll share it."

"No, thanks. I'll eat something later, back at the house." He gulped back almost half of the pint of beer in one go and lit a cigarette.

Before we had the sandwiches eaten, Oscar had another pint of lager sitting in front of him. "Are you sure you won't have a beer now that you've almost finished your coffee, Johnny?"

"No, thanks. Drink makes me sleepy in the middle of the day."

"How about you, Nome?"

Naomi's face darkened. "You know well I have to pick up the boys from school in a couple of hours. I don't want to be fuzzy headed driving."

Oscar drank the second pint in less than five minutes, then got to his feet. "Be back in a minute. Just going to the lav."

Naomi watched him leaving the lounge. "He's been a bit anxious over the last few days. I think it's the recording sessions coming up. He was off the drink for months awhile back, but he always loved a pint or two at lunchtime."

I nodded. "How are the two boys doing at school?"

Naomi sat up. "Fine. Fintan gets into trouble with his teacher occasionally, but everyone loves Mark. He gets away with murder."

"They're nice boys."

Naomi squeezed her hands. "Fintan can be difficult at times. He wasn't always like that. When Oscar gave up photography and started the band last year, it had a big effect on him. He hated it when he was away on long tours. But Oscar says that once you get a recording deal the band won't need to tour so much."

I nodded, though I couldn't see how this could be true.

We sat in silence for a few moments; then Naomi turned to me. "By the way, I know someone who may be able to rent you a room when you move over here permanently. It's that friend of mine I was telling Oscar about earlier, Vivian. She has a house here in Chiswick with a few of the upper rooms converted into self-contained bedsits. She's just after breaking up with her partner, so she'll be strapped for cash. I'll suggest it to her, if you like?"

"I'd appreciate it. My girlfriend may be coming over, too, if I can persuade her to give up her job."

"Viv would have no problem with that. The rooms may not be all that great, though. She lets them mainly to students. But it would do till you find something more suitable." Naomi glanced towards the door leading to the toilets. "I wonder what's keeping Oscar; he's been gone a long time."

I got to my feet. "I'll see if I can find him. I need to go to the toilet anyway."

There was no sign of Oscar in the men's room. I went to the bar at the back of the premises and looked through the glass-panelled door. Oscar was standing at the counter with a cigarette in his mouth and a half-empty glass in his hand.

THE ROOM

The room was shabby and it was bare
But when you came and joined me there
You turned it into a home, didn't you, Joan?
THE ROOM

HE JUKEBOX IN the corner started playing 'Midnight at the Oasis' for the fourth or fifth time since we'd entered the lounge. Joan sipped her lager and sang along with the song.

I laughed at her tuneless voice. "I wonder who keeps playing that song?"

Joan gazed past me. "I think it's that girl with the long floral dress back there. The dark-haired one. She's been going over and back to the jukebox all night."

I glanced over my shoulder and noticed a girl roughly the same age as Joan. "You mean the attractive looking one with the long black hair who looks a bit like you?"

Joan glanced back at the girl. "She's much prettier than me. I used to wear those long dresses, but they're gone out of fashion now."

I looked at Joan's polka-dot slimline top and matching flimsy skirt, an outfit she'd bought in Chelsea a few days after arriving in London some weeks before. "Don't be so modest. You look terrific."

Joan lowered her eyes. "You don't think this blouse is too revealing, do you? I was going to wear my green one."

I looked at the low-cut neckline of her cotton blouse, and my eyes lingered on the shadow of her cleavage. "No, the white shows up your tan really well. You look great. And I'm not the only one who thinks so. That guy over there in the black jacket has been gaping at you all night. I'll have to be careful."

Joan glanced across the room at the fella I was talking about. "We'll go after this drink, if you like. You're rehearsing again tomorrow, aren't you? Maybe you'd like an early night?"

"No, no, you like it here. We'll stay. I don't have to be at Oscar's till after one. But don't remind me of that. I had another terrible row with him today."

"Over what?"

"Musical differences, what else? I don't know how I'll ever last singing his songs for five years."

"Why five years?"

"That's the term of the recording contract we're going to have to sign. I can always opt out at some stage, but there'll be a clawback clause for anyone who leaves the band before the end of the term. I don't want to end up in debt to a record company."

Joan had no interest in my business affairs. She took her purse from her bag. "If we're staying, we'd better get another drink. I'll get this round."

"No, no, I'll get it. I'm not that badly off yet."

We left the bar at closing time and strolled up the main street. Though it was late September, it was still very warm. After the drinks, Joan was a little tipsy. She did a twirl on the pavement and started singing 'Midnight at the Oasis'. I put my hand around her slim waist and started kissing her. She held my neck and pressed against me. After a few moments, she broke away from my mouth and smiled. "That was nice."

I took her hand. "You've changed a lot since you moved over here, do you know that?"

"In what way?"

"You seem a lot freer in yourself. Maybe it's the insecurity. You're like a tightrope walker working without a net for the first time. Your net being the net income of the secure job you gave up to throw in your lot with a struggling clown like me."

Joan laughed. "How do you know that it wasn't your big recording deal that lured me?"

"Because that hasn't come off yet. And anyway, it isn't my deal; it's Oscar's."

We arrived at the house just before twelve. To avoid meeting Viv, our in-house landlady, we tiptoed up the two flights of stairs to our bedsit. The moment I opened the room door a strong smell of gas made me gag. "We forgot to open the window again before going out."

I switched on the light. The room was tiny, with peeling wallpaper and very basic furnishings – a Formica table, two iron chairs, a lopsided wardrobe, a rusty pre-war gas cooker and a single bed.

I raised the window to let in some fresh air, then went to the cooker and twisted the control knobs to the off position. Joan watched me with an amused look on her face. "You do that every night, but it's no good. There must be a leaking pipe somewhere. You're going to have to ask her again to get it fixed. It's bound to be bad for our health."

"It's fine when we keep the window open."

Joan raised her eyebrows. "But it's almost October. What are we going to do when the cold weather comes?"

I took off my jacket and threw it across the back of one of the chairs. "I'll say it to her tomorrow before I go to rehearsals. But I don't think it'll do any good. I've said it to her before. We'll just have to move out of here when the advance money from the record company comes through."

I took a packet of Bisodol tablets from my pocket and put one in my mouth. Joan noticed me sucking it. "Is your stomach at you again?"

"A little."

"You worry too much. Even in the pub you couldn't stop thinking about Oscar and the band. You need to switch off sometime."

I rubbed my stomach. "I wish I could."

Joan took off her jacket and put it in the wardrobe; then she went to the open window and stuck her head out. "Mmmm, there's a lovely smell coming from the garden next door. Apples and roses. It reminds me of home. I always loved the smell from the fields and orchards back in Galway at this time of the year. A bit like this. Come and smell."

I went to the window and put my head out. "It's lovely."

Joan looked over the rooftops of some nearby houses. "Look, the moon is on its back. A sure sign of rain."

I raised my eyes. "There's very few clouds in the sky."

Joan sniffed the air. "I can smell it. It's coming all right. Lots of signs forecast the weather. Sheep go to higher ground and cattle move close to bushes and trees before it rains."

"You won't find many of them in London."

Joan laughed. Her face was propped in the palms of her hands with her elbows leaning on the windowsill. I touched her cheek. "You miss home, do you?"

"I don't miss Dublin. It just feels a little strange being so far away from Galway. Not that I went home that often. But it was always there, just a train ride away. Here it's different."

I touched her temple. "It was a huge sacrifice you made, giving up your job and coming over here."

Joan smiled. "I have no regrets."

I ran the back of my hand down her cheek and then slid my fingers through her hair just below her ear. Her mouth opened slightly. A crooked tooth that she was in the habit of concealing with her upper lip became visible. I touched it with the tip of my finger. She smiled and the tooth became more exposed. I leaned over and we started kissing. In the middle of the kiss, the plumbing beneath the sink started rattling, as it often did when anyone in the house used the taps. Though we were used to the noise, Joan's neck jerked upwards and she banged the crown of her head against the edge of the upper window frame. She cursed and moved back into the room, laughing and rubbing her scalp.

"Are you OK?"

"Fine. You might mention that to her tomorrow as well. What a place!"

The rattling stopped. I went and sat on the bed.

In the middle of the room, Joan took off her skirt and started opening the front of her blouse. "It's so warm. It's like a summer's night." She put the blouse and skirt on a hanger in the wardrobe, then went back to the open window in her slip and raised her arms to let the air get at her underarms. "I love it when it's like this, when you don't have to wear much clothes and you still feel comfortable." She started singing 'Midnight at the Oasis' again.

I kicked off my desert boots and sat back on the bed. "You're brain-washed with that blasted song. Why don't you sing one of mine for a change?"

Joan smiled and started singing an old song of mine, swaying her head to the waltz tempo of the tune: *I want to try and say all that I have to say, for it's the only way you'll know about me. . .* She stopped singing but kept rocking her head backwards and forwards. "That's my favourite song of yours." She sang another line: *You need some time to think on things that I say, I need to know the truth about you and me. . .*

I couldn't help laughing at her wobbly voice. She stopped singing abruptly. "I know I can't sing. More than anything in the world I'd love to have a good voice. I used to dream of singing on stage when I was young."

"You have other talents."

"Like what?"

"You're a teacher, aren't you? And you're good at decorating."

"What do you mean?"

I looked at the yellow curtains and the coordinating yellow eiderdown I was sitting on. "You've made a great job of this place since you came here. I used to hate coming back here before you arrived."

Joan looked around the room. "It isn't too bad now, I suppose. I'll never forget the shock I got when I first came here. How did you live like that?"

"I didn't come here that often, just to sleep."

Joan went to the sink and brushed her teeth. While she was drying her mouth, she noticed one of my socks lying on the floor near the table. She bent to pick it up. Her slip rose a few inches on her thigh. The tendons and muscles at the back of her leg bulged and stretched. She sensed that I was watching her. With her head down, she looked back at me through the falling strands of her long dark hair and smiled. "What are you looking at?"

"Come here."

She put the sock in a plastic bag. "Will I turn out the light?"

"Yeah, but leave the curtains open for the fresh air."

She switched out the light and got into bed. I took off my jeans and shirt and got in beside her.

Because the bed was so narrow, it was a tight squeeze lying side by side. Joan rested her knee over on my leg and lay close to me with her hand on my chest. "Tickle my arm, will you; slowly, the way I like it."

233

I ran the tips of my fingers along the inside of her arm. I could feel her veins with the back of my thumb.

"That's nice." She pushed up my vest and ran the palm of her hand over my ribcage. "I'll rub your stomach. It might help you relax."

"I am relaxed."

"No, you're not. Your muscles are all tensed up down here in your stomach. That's where you get the pain, isn't it?"

"Around there."

"Is it paining you now?"

"A little."

Joan massaged my stomach. "If you're not happy in the band, why don't you leave them?"

I sat up in the bed. "Are you joking? I couldn't do that!"

"Why not?"

"How would we live?"

"Maybe you'd get a deal by yourself. You said it was your songs that the company liked."

"Yeah, but Oscar was the one who got them to take us on. I have no guarantee that they'd want to work with me if I left the band."

Joan sat up beside me. "Why don't you ask them?"

I hesitated. "I've thought about it, but I wouldn't like going behind Oscar's back. If I left the band, he'd probably lose the recording deal. I'd hate to be responsible for that."

"I'm sure he'd find a replacement singer."

I drew a deep breath. "I don't know. It would be very risky."

Joan ran her hand across my stomach. "You said earlier that working without a net had changed me for the better. Maybe it would free you up, too."

I laughed.

Joan slid back into a lying position. I moved down in the bed beside her and put my knee over her leg. The skin of her thigh was smooth and silky. We started kissing.

JOYFUL MYSTERY

When we moved to the country
After the deal fell through
It wasn't easy for a city boy like me
I'm lucky I had you
I'M LUCKY I HAD YOU

A SHARP PAIN in my stomach woke me just before dawn. My mouth filled up with bile. I hopped out of bed and rushed to the fireplace and spat into the grate. Again my mouth filled up with the sour liquid, and again I spewed it out. I reached for a bottle of Maalox on the mantelpiece and took a swig; then I went back and got under the covers. Within seconds I was free of the pain.

I tried to go back to sleep, but a calf lowing in one of the barns at the back of the cottage kept me awake. I switched on my bedside lamp and took up a paperback copy of James Joyce's *Dubliners* and started reading. An hour went by. Joan's parents, Tom and Nora, started stirring in the room above me. A few minutes later, they came downstairs. I could hear them shuffling around in the living room and kitchen, taking out the ashes and starting the fires. Eventually Tom went off to the fields for the cows and Nora left to feed the hens.

I became so engrossed in the story I was reading I didn't hear Joan coming downstairs. She opened the door of my room and stuck her head in. "You're awake?"

I put the book down. "I couldn't sleep with that blasted calf. Listen, it's still moaning out there."

Joan came into the room. "The poor thing. Daddy separated it from its mother yesterday. It takes them ages to get over being parted like that. How're you feeling this morning?"

"Better than yesterday. That was a good idea of yours of going to the pub last night. It took me out of myself. But I shouldn't have had that extra pint at the end of the night. It upset my stomach."

Joan came over to the bed and touched the side of my face. "The swelling around your eye has gone down anyway, I see. You're going to have to go to a doctor with that if it swells up again. That's the third time it's happened this month. It must be some kind of an allergy you've developed."

I leaned up and kissed Joan on the mouth. "It's nothing a good night with you wouldn't cure. I was going to creep up to you last night, but I kept hearing footsteps upstairs."

Joan pulled away from me nervously. "I'm glad you didn't. That was Daddy. He was up and down the stairs all night. There was a cow calving in the near field. She dropped around five in the morning. Daddy didn't get a wink of sleep with her."

I got out of bed and started dressing. "I had a bad night's sleep myself. Dreams kept waking me. In one Oscar and his son Fintan were chasing me through a field. I tripped over a stone and cut my head. Oscar and Fintan caught up with me and started laughing. Then Oscar put a clarinet to his mouth and began to play."

"Strange dream."

"The stone I tripped over might have something to do with the way things have gone wrong for me since I left the Brewery. The dream might be my subconscious way of letting Oscar win out for the bad conscience I was left with after walking out on him."

Joan laughed and looked at her watch. "You and your subconscious! I'd better hurry. Fr Michael's calling to the school this morning to examine the communion class. He's expecting a definite answer from me today about whether I'm going to stay on at the school permanently. I've been putting him off now for months. What will I tell him?"

I hesitated. "I suppose you'd better say you're staying. It doesn't look like we'll be going to LA at this stage, does it?"

Joan looked at me. "I can always hand in my notice again if you get word from your producer."

"Don't hold your breath."

I took out the ashes and set a turf fire in my room; then I joined Joan for breakfast in the dining room. While we were eating, Nora arrived in from her chores. She was wearing an odd pair of wellington boots and a thread-bare cardigan. She smiled at Joan. "Musha, you have the tay made, a girleen. I told himself you need to be at school a biteen earlier today, so he'll drive you down before he has his breakfast. He's running late on account of the calf droppin'." She turned to me. "And how's your lordship this mornin'? Did you get the night all right, a grá?"

"Not bad, Nora. How about yourself?"

"Musha, don't be talkin'. Himself had me awake all night comin' and goin' with that blashted beast. You'd think she'd be more considerate and have her calf at a reasonable hour."

After breakfast, Tom drove Joan to school in his Morris Minor, and Nora went off to take the cows back to the fields. I returned to my room and read a few pages of Dylan Thomas's *Under Milk Wood.*

At nine-thirty I put the book down and got out a hand written manu-script of an autobiography I had worked on all winter while waiting to hear from a producer who had taken some recordings of mine to America. I had started working on the memoir to try and unravel some of the con-fusion I felt about my career in the music business, but I soon discovered that I had little or no talent for writing prose. The manuscript was a mess. I had abandoned it several times but kept coming back to it for want of anything better to do.

I started to read one of the early chapters now. It began with a descrip-tion of the street in Limerick where I grew up and went on to describe some of the characters I knew as a boy. After reading a few pages, I began to feel a terrible sense of weariness at the flatness of the prose. I threw the manuscript on the bed and confronted myself in the mirror above the mantelpiece. "You're no Joyce or Thomas, that's for sure!"

I lit a cigarette and went to the window. Outside it was grey and over-cast. I looked down past Quinn's farm towards the forestry. On first arriving in the village almost a year before, this view of the woods had taken my breath away.

Now my eyes focused on the graveyard to the side of the trees, where some jackdaws were hovering above the gravestones.

After I finished smoking the cigarette, I took my guitar from its case and tuned it. A melody I'd come up with a week or so earlier came into my head. It was a simple air structured around three major chords. I had tried writing a song around it a few days before, but it failed to take off. One of the lines I'd come up with back then came into my head. I sang it: *When I stabbed you in the back did the child feel the pain?* It sounded contrived and melodramatic. I spent twenty minutes trying to find an alternative starting point, without success. In frustration, I threw the guitar on the bed and spat into the fire.

The postman's van pulled up outside the cottage. A few minutes later, Nora tapped on my door and handed me a letter. "I hope it's good news."

"I hope so, too, Nora. Thanks."

The letter turned out to be one I had sent to Los Angeles myself six or seven weeks earlier. I tore open the envelope and read my own hand written note to my record producer:

> Dear Tony
> My last letter to you was returned unopened. I hope this one will have better luck in reaching you. Regarding my rejection of you offer: I must state again that I couldn't possibly agree to give you 50% of the publishing rights to my songs. I've never heard of a record producer asking for such a thing! If you had told me you were going to expect such a cut at the outset I would never have agreed to it. Now that you have a company over there interested in doing a deal, surely it's in both our interests to find a resolution to this problem? Please wire me a contact number so that I can phone you.
>
> > Anxiously yours,

I threw the letter on the bed and reached for the Maalox on the mantelpiece. After taking a swig, I went to the window. The sky had brightened a little above the graveyard. I decided to go for my morning walk a little earlier than usual to try and clear my head.

The moment I stepped out the back door, an oatmeal-coloured Labrador came bounding across the farmyard towards me, flapping its head from side to side.

"Morning, Sancho." I looked at the dog's right ear. Part of it had been bitten off by one of the mongrel sheepdogs from the village a few days earlier, and it still hadn't healed. I went back into the house and got some ointment and put it on the raw wound. "We should never have brought you here, Sancho. You'll never survive."

I set off with the dog at my heels.

Going by the barnyard, I spotted Tom shovelling manure from one of the cowsheds. "Do you need a hand at that, Tom?"

Tom doffed his cap. "No, but I might need you tomorrow to help with some ploughin' up in the far field, if the rain howlds off."

I nodded. "You know where I'll be."

"I do, *a grá*. Enjoy your walk."

Past the hayshed I came to the end of the tarmacadamed part of the road. In front of me a dirt path wound its bumpy way between fields bordered with elder and hawthorn trees on one side and a stone wall and rusty barbed-wire fencing on the other side. The path itself was rutted with deep cart tracks and potholes. The moment I stepped off the tarmac, I realised I had made a mistake in not putting on wellington boots before setting out. Recent rain had turned the dips and ruts into pools of mud and muck. To try and keep my desert boots clean, I walked along the grass margin.

Outside the village, I looked up towards the sloping fields on my right. They were dull and bare now, but back in the summer I had helped Tom work them when they were a rich green colour. Memories came back to me of cutting and saving hay, mowing and gathering oats, digging and picking potatoes, footing and stacking turf.

After walking for ten or fifteen minutes, I came to a small pond on the edge of a wide bog. Miles of heathery shrubland spread all the way to the horizon on one side of the water, and a dense wood surrounded the other side. I threw a stick out into the centre of the pond, and Sancho swam out to retrieve it.

While I was waiting for the dog to return with the stick, I started thinking about the manuscript back in my room. I called to mind the hometown chapter and wondered how I hadn't managed to bring it to life in my prose. While I was trying to figure out what the missing ingredient was, I started humming a tune. I didn't recognise the air at first, but then it came to me that it was the same melody I had worked on earlier back at the cottage. While I was humming it, I began to feel that there was a connection between the resonance of the tune and the atmosphere of the street I had grown up in. After this dawned on me, I realised that the street scene would make a good song. I scratched my head, puzzled that I hadn't thought of this before.

As soon as Sancho emerged from the water, I hurried back to my room and started re-reading the early chapter. A few incidents from the first few pages caught my attention. I got down to work and edited them down to a couple of verses:

> The old spinster is going insane
> Her next-door neighbour is in church again
> Two drunks are fighting down in the lane
> While little children are playing a game
>
> Dogs are barking, little girls sing
> And the chapel bell begins to ring
> Someone deals Bobby a king
> On the pavement money starts to ring

The old spinster was a neighbour of ours whose widowed father (it was said) had refused to let her marry when she was in her twenties because he couldn't face the thought of living alone. The singing children, ringing church bells and barking dogs were common sounds in our neighbourhood, and I was delighted to include one of my earliest friends, Bobby, playing street poker in the second verse.

After rooting around for some more ideas, I came up with another couple of verses:

> The cripple crawls up the avenue
> Someone else says, "How do you do"
> Someone kicks a ball over to you
> While the sky begins to lose its hue

> A group of old stevedores from the ships
> Come up the street bent from the hips
> One takes a cigarette from his lips
> Another catches the coin he flips

While I was developing these lines, I imagined I was back in the old street sitting on the pavement with my back against Began's gable-end wall watching the characters I was portraying. Mr Mac was an old stroke victim who exercised on his wobbly crutches each evening while kids played ball and groups of stevedores from the docks passed along the street.

While I was singing these verses, a chorus melody grew out of the main melodic line, and words formed around it effortlessly like tendrils growing on one of the garden fences along the street. When it was completed it stood out like the flower of the song:

> And the street is drifting into evening
> While the sun is going down
> I'm just back there capturing the feeling
> Though it's just another town

Joan arrived home from school just after four. When she saw I was busy with a song, she made me some coffee and let me get on with it. Two more verses came to me during the following hour:

> The old nurse is on her way to the shop
> The epileptic suddenly drops
> Down the hill my father's in the docks
> In the bars the drinking never stops
>
> Bobby throws down a pair of queens
> The church bell interrupts someone's dreams
> Someone's talking of football teams
> Some girl is straightening her nylon seams

I felt good about including my father in the song, and I brought Bobby and the church bells back to give the lyric a sense of continuity. Rounding the whole thing off with the girl fixing her stockings was just a light, cheeky touch to add a little humour to the ending.

I broke for dinner and returned to my room just after six to work on the vocal phrasing. Joan stuck her head round the door a couple of hours later and raised her eyebrows. "Still at it?!"

"I'm almost finished now. Will I sing it for you?"

Joan looking at her watch. "Mammy and Daddy are just about to start the rosary. Are you coming out? You can sing it for me later."

I looked at the clock on the mantelpiece. It was almost eight, the family's customary time for saying the rosary. Though I felt hypocritical about taking part in this ritual each evening, I did it for Joan's sake. But tonight I was reluctant to leave my new song.

"Couldn't you make some excuse for me for once?"

Joan looked at me. "I don't want to offend them. Do it for me, please! It won't kill you."

I drew a loud breath and got to my feet.

In the living room, Tom and Nora were already on their knees with rosary beads in their hands. In the corner above the TV set, a red votive lamp was burning below a picture of the Sacred Heart. Beside it a statue of Our Lady stood lopsided on a tilting shelf with a pair of glittering rosary beds around its neck.

Joan and I got down on our knees and joined our hands. Tom started the first decade of the rosary in his usual speedy fashion, making one long word out of the first half of the prayer: "OurFatherwhoartinheavenHallowedbeThynameThykingdomcomeThywillbedoneonearthasitisinheaven."

Nora began the response more slowly, and Joan and I joined in: "Give us this day our daily bread and forgive us our trespasses as we forgive those who trespass against us. Lead us not into temptation and deliver us from evil, amen."

"HailMaryfullofgraceTheLordiswiththeeBlessedartthouamongstwomen . . ."

"Holy Mary, mother of God, pray for us sinners. . ."

As the decade droned on, I went on automatic and started thinking about some of the disturbed and maimed characters I had written about in my new song. I began to wonder what had made me focus on them. While I was pondering this question, a boyhood memory came back to me. I was walking with my mother down our street when we passed by a boy with a lame leg from the neighbourhood. I was so lost in my own thoughts I hardly saw him till my mother pulled me up. "That boy in the foot-brace smiled at you, and you didn't even notice him!" I tried to excuse myself by explaining that I had been thinking about something important, but my mother shook her head firmly. "There's nothing more important than being aware of people around you."

Another Hail Mary came to an end. I looked across the room at Tom. His gnarled, work-worn fingers moved to another bead. I didn't have any of his devotion or faith, but for once it seemed appropriate to be on my knees, reciting the first Joyful Mystery.